FIND IT. GROW IT. KEEP IT.

DISCOVER THE SECRET WEALTH INSIDE YOUR BUSINESS AND NAVIGATE YOUR WAY TO AFFLUENT PROSPERITY

NICK SMITH

Find It. Grow It. Keep It. Discover the Secret Wealth Inside Your Business and Navigate Your Way to Affluent Prosperity

First Edition (2021)

ISBN: 978-1-8383853-0-9

Published by The Financial Navigator

www.thefinancialnavigator.co.uk

Cover design: Jadine Rice of Kay Flawless Ltd.

www.kayflawless.com

CONTENTS

DISCLAIMER

As you would expect, I work in a highly regulated industry and we live in a litigious society, so I need to point some things out to you.

I'm not an accountant and I'm not a tax adviser.

This book represents my personal opinions and thoughts and does not constitute financial advice.

Past performance is not indicative of future performance. The value of your investment and any income from it may go down as well as up. You may not get back the original amount you invested.

The levels and bases of taxation and reliefs from taxation can change at any time. Tax relief depends on individual circumstances.

An investment in equities and shares will not provide the security of capital associated with a deposit account with a bank or building society.

Tax and estate planning services are not regulated by the Financial Conduct Authority.

Please bear in mind that the book references some endnotes throughout—you should read them for your own clarity.

FOREWORD

When Nick first asked me to write something for his book I was terrified.

I imagined endless, dry pages detailing accountancy procedures or, alternatively, some sort of aggressive American-style financial self-help bible bullying the reader into shouting positive slogans at themselves in the mirror every morning.

I worried that my world—music—was so far removed from his that I couldn't possibly comment on something that was obviously beyond my sphere of expertise. Well, that's why we have financial advisors, right?

The inevitable truth, though, was that this book was a far more engaging and thoughtful read than I anticipated.

Instead of being some pumped-up manual for success, I found it surprisingly reflective and philosophical. Yes, he draws many parallels with his experiences in the Navy, but they never come across as bullish. The anecdotes, rather than being simple war stories, seem more like parables and tend to invite interesting debates about the nature of risk.

I particularly enjoyed Nick's reflections on the purpose of failure, something with which I have become increasingly fascinated as I look back at my own career arc.

As a financial consultant, Nick provides wise guidance and a sense of protection—and, fittingly, this book resonates with a similar kind of aegis and ultimately reveals itself to be quietly and unexpectedly inspirational.

Brett Anderson, January 2021

THE BIG MINDSET SECRET

I asked two fundamental questions when I set out to write this book: why am I writing it and who is it for? It turns out it's really hard to write a book, unless you're someone like Stephen King. The very thought of having to write sixty or seventy thousand words would fill most people with dread. It certainly did for me.

Without a good reason to do all this work (because it is a *lot* of work), there's no way I could have done this. I'll come to my reason in a moment.

Before I do, though, here's a note on mindset. You'll find much about mindset in this book, for an excellent reason: everything happens in your head before anything happens outside it.

Take this book, and the mindset I was in when I first started out. Look at the words I was using: "*have to*". I "had to" write sixty thousand words.

How about, instead, I decide I *get to* write a book. How lucky am I?

The reality, like many big projects, is a sixty thousand word book starts with just one word. And then another. And then three. Before you know it, you're at ten thousand, twenty thousand—and you're in a flow. Sure, there are good days and bad days, distracted days and clear-thinking days.

But that's okay.

Get into a routine, get the support and accountability you need (thank you Vicky at Moxie Books), and get writing. To do so, I needed the right mindset.

If I "have" to write, I won't enjoy it, it'll take forever, and it'll be a pile of steaming dog poo. A different mindset will lead to a different outcome: if I "get" to write a book, that's exciting. I'll enjoy it, I'll get a great deal out of it, my enthusiasm will shine through in my writing, and my book will make a difference to at least one person's life: mine.

If I write with enthusiasm, my book will be helpful and informative and it'll help the people who read it make positive change in their lives.

Which brings me neatly to my reasons for doing this. I wrote this book because I want to help people build a stable financial future, despite everything that may be going on in the world. I'm driven by the difference I make to people's real lives. That I get paid for it is a happy by-product.

Take one of my lovely clients. He was self-employed and earning £120,000 and his partner was earning £20,000 in part-time employment. They're a couple in their mid-to-late fifties, married with grown-up children, living in a modest home with a small-ish mortgage. I expected them to be in a decent position.

Never judge a book by its cover…

They had high-interest unsecured debt (credit cards) and personal loans, no budget plan, and no retirement savings plan. They didn't know where they were spending their money nor what they could do about it.

As the COVID-19 lockdown hit in March 2020, I called my clients to make sure they were okay and to see if there was anything I could do to reassure them. Like most of us, they were scared. They both had underlying health issues, his income dried up overnight, and he wasn't eligible for any meaningful government support. They were genuinely worried about what would happen.

But they were also very grateful. They were grateful for the structure and financial measures we had put in place only 12 months before, without which they would have been well up the proverbial creek. They had savings to weather the storm. Their debt was consolidated and manageable. They had a budget. They knew they could manage for an entire year without income, which was a considerable improvement on the one month they could have survived previously. My clients were still scared, but the financial worry had diminished.

There is no greater reward than the gift of giving, which is why I wrote this book.

I get to give my knowledge and experience to help business owners achieve personal sovereignty and affluent prosperity. I get to help clients understand money, and how small changes can make a big difference. I get to help young people appreciate long-term savings and know that when they reach retirement age, when the state will not be there for them like it is for us and our parents, they will be okay. They will have enough.

I get to give, and that is wonderful.

But not everybody is ready to receive. Most business owners know they need help; someone to talk to about their business to help them make decisions and focus on what they can control. But they'll be ready for that help when they're ready, and not when I think they should be ready.

So I wrote this book for those business owners, to help them get ready.

This isn't a book about numbers, and you'll find no financial advice within. It's a book full of information and lessons I've learned over the years that have helped me transform my business into a profitable machine that works for me, instead of a drain on my time, energy, and resources.

Now, you might think that means my pockets are brimming with cash. That's simply not the case, because my profit-making machine does just enough for me and no more. I don't want jet skis, speedboats, and properties abroad. I don't want Armani suits, jewellery, and the latest expensive consumer gadgets.

(Actually, I do like gadgets, so I do have some of those.)

Instead, I want freedom. I want personal sovereignty and affluent prosperity. I want enough time and enough money to allow me to enjoy my freedom, to do what I want, when I want. That is the essence of personal sovereignty and affluent prosperity: the freedom to choose. That freedom doesn't come easy. It takes hard work, commitment, and energy, but it is eminently doable and within your reach–if you truly commit to it.

In this book, you'll read my story: how I uncovered myself, how I overcame my limiting beliefs, and how I built a business that helps people and rewards me, financially and emotionally.

Thank you for choosing to read it. I hope you find it interesting, enjoyable, and it makes a positive difference to your life.

I am 100 percent emotionally invested in the impact this book has on you. I'm excited to hear your story, to understand where you are now and where you arrive at the end of this book. I can't wait to hear it.

So please, let me know. Tell me how you feel about your business right now. Is it chewing up your cash, swallowing all your energy, and spitting out dribbles? Is it chugging along but not really igniting your passion? Or is it setting the world on fire?

Email me here–nick@thefinancialnavigator.co.uk–and share your story as it is today. Then read the book and tell me what's changed. I'd love to hear from you.

Enjoy!

Nick Smith

The Financial Navigator

p.s. You'll not be added to any mailing list by emailing your story. I promise.

INTRODUCTION: MAYDAY! MAYDAY! MAYDAY!

"Lynx helicopter, two persons on board, fire in the cabin, emergency landing."

Repeat.

Land (quickly).

Run.

Light cigarette.

We were on the ground within 60 seconds of sending the Mayday call, probably less, as we were low-flying at one hundred feet.

Few aircrews, be they military or civilian, ever give a Mayday call and live to tell the tale.

I know risk. I have a unique understanding of its nature. And I know that expertise, experience, and training prepares us for unexpected emergencies (like a fire in the cabin of my helicopter).

But what on earth does an ex-Naval aviator know about business and financial advice? It's a good question which I answer with this: I've discovered how to apply the lessons I learned in the Navy to my business, so I can build affluent prosperity for myself and for my clients.

We think of the military as something unique and

abnormal but it really isn't. Most of the work is about leadership and management, the same as in business. In the Navy, the client is your superior officer. You have a budget. You have tools and resources. You invest in training and team-building. Yes, the environment is unique at times, but the work and the results are not much different. There are exceptions, of course: war, humanitarian operations, counter-terrorism, search and rescue, to name a few.

But ultimately, the same skills are required to run a successful business as to run a successful military operation.

The captain of a warship is running a 200-strong business for UK plc. Leadership, management, logistics, budgets, discipline, policies, procedures, training, marketing[1], communication, facilities management, IT... the list goes on.

I'll come back to business in a moment. First, I want to take you back into the cockpit with me and tell you a little more about that emergency landing, because I want you to understand where I'm coming from and why I'm writing this book.

I Know Risk

We're on a fighter evasion sortie with two RAF Tornados near Oban in north-west Scotland. We're low-flying at 100 feet and 150 miles per hour along the valleys and lochs, with the Tornados flying at 500 feet and 600 miles an hour, trying to "shoot" us. Our job: evade. Don't die. The Tornado pilots report on whether our evasion tactics would keep us alive in a real combat situation.

You have to keep your wits about you at 100 feet. Total focus and concentration. Working together as a team. Pilot: eyes out, keeping us away from the ground, avoiding obstacles (pylons and wires), eyes out for the fighter jets. Observer (navigator—me, more on that later): eyes out for the Tornados, eyes out for obstacles, eyes in on the temperatures and pressures for anything untoward. Oh, and navigate: I need to know where we are at all times and make sure we don't run out of fuel.

You need a cool head under pressure. The ability to make clear decisions in highly complex environments. Clear communication. Razor-sharp senses.

We're properly throwing the aircraft around. Despite the obvious risks at 100 feet and 150 miles per hour, and the intense concentration, it's great fun. I'm 24 years old on my first tour out of flying training, preparing to deploy to the Gulf.

I am having a ball.

Until, after one manoeuvre, we smell burning in the cockpit. The alternator warning light flashes on—but there's no other abnormal temperature or pressure indicators. Flying along the northern bank of Loch Etive, we make a decision: time for a precautionary landing.

We radio the Tornados and land on the beach-cum-front garden of a house on the banks of the loch (Lord knows what the inhabitants thought of a Lynx helicopter on their front lawn). I jump out and look around: nothing amiss. The smell's gone and the alternator light has gone out.

No reason to hang around: we take off, inform the Tornados we're ready to get back into the chase, and head south across the loch to continue the exercise.

Feet dry (back over dry land)—and the light and smell are back, suffocating this time. I turn to find thick black acrid smoke pouring into the back of the aircraft through the sound insulation—with flames visible through the smoke.

That's when the training kicked in. The hours of simulated emergencies. Teamwork. Clear decision-making. The value of expertise.

We didn't need to discuss it. We knew exactly what to do. We acted. Self-preservation, I suppose:

Harness.

Radio.

Brace.

Partial crash checks.

No need to turn the engines off… yet.

Lock the harness, put out the Mayday call, brace for impact.

Grab the fire extinguisher from the back of the pilot's seat. Pull my short-term air supply bottle from my lifejacket.

Open the window: we can't see out of the cockpit windows through the thick smoke.

It was all over in less than 60 seconds, but it remains carved into my memory.

We landed, rapidly.

We switched everything off, rapidly.

We applied the emergency rotor brake, rapidly.

We got out, rapidly.

I lit a cigarette with shaking hands. Less rapidly.

And had time to look around.

The smoke had stopped. What we thought was fire, we realised was the orange winch hook (for search and rescue work) just glimpsed through the smoke.

We were alive. And so was UK plc's multi-million pound helicopter.

Better let our colleagues know all was well: they'd had no contact with us for several minutes after our Mayday call and now had no contact with us following a precautionary landing a few minutes earlier. Good thing we did: the Tornados had put out a Mayday Relay call which had launched the search and rescue helicopter from Prestwick (about 20 minutes flying time away) and alerted local police units to look for us.[2]

So yes, I know risk.

I also know you need expertise to manage risk.

Only an expert gets to do what I did for a living.

By the same token, only an expert knows how to manage the financial consequences of risk for you, your family, and your business. You wouldn't let just anyone fly the plane, would you?

Quick Thinking

During my service in the Arabian Gulf and Far East, aged 24, I was responsible for a team of eight aircraft engineers in challenging and arduous conditions. I've hosted defence sales days in the Far East, schmoozed dignitaries at cocktail parties around the world, visited schools and air shows, and hosted stands at all kinds of events. Not all were great fun, I can assure you. I learned to be the most interesting person at the party by asking questions and saying little about myself. I have some great stories from that time, some of which I'll share in this book, but one of my most abiding memories had nothing to do with risk.

One of the aircraft engineers came to see me one morning and said, "Boss, I've got a bit of a problem." He placed a stack of envelopes on my desk and explained that he was being chased by the Child Support Agency following an unintended pregnancy from a short-lived romance. I was 24, he was 28, I was green and naïve, and I didn't have the faintest clue what to do. But I knew how to listen and empathise, and I committed to help him. We sorted things out together, and I made sure he dealt with the matter rather than burying his head in the sand.

I did what I said I would do. Like Ronseal.

Every time I face something new in my business, which is often, I think back to that time. I recognise that I don't always need the answer at my fingertips. Having the skills to empathise, listen, and understand is more important than throwing out a quick answer and sending someone away.

Leadership is about making time for your team, putting their thoughts and feelings first, and making sure they feel special. Because they are. You and your business are nothing without your team (even if you're a solopreneur—none of us can do this alone).

The military taught me many things, but I have picked out five I think are most relevant to my business experience:

- Listen to others.
- Value expertise.
- Understand risk.
- Know your worth.
- Do what you say you're going to do.

I don't know everything—not even close—which is why I have a mentor and a coach, and why I read a lot. I also don't know what I don't know. And that's okay, too.

I have started and failed in as many businesses in my early entrepreneurial days as I have had success more recently. I have had failures in security, parking, and recruitment. I have had success in consultancy, recruitment, property and, of course, financial advice.

I could not have had the success without the failures. The failures are as much a part of me as the wins.

So yes, I know risk. I've taken many risks in the past, some of which led to failure and some of which led to success. The key thing is to learn from all of them so we can build the business and life we dream of.

Affluent Prosperity

We all want it. Affluent prosperity, sustainable wealth, a richer lifestyle, and an enduring legacy.

Few people achieve it.

Some only dream it.

Most never make it.

The reason most people only dream and struggle to achieve what they want is a simple mindset error.

Because you *can* do it.

The problem is most business owners equate achieving more with doing more. More work, more time, more hours, more risk, more commitment. They think this is the only way to achieve financial stability and the "success" they crave. And for some that does indeed work, but it always comes at a cost. Broken marriages, children's lost childhood, alcohol problems.

What use is lonely wealth?

Instead, I want to help you build success on your terms, whatever it looks like to you.

This book will show you how to achieve affluent prosperity with less effort, less stress, and less fear.

You can do it. Yes, you can.

If you are:

- Willing and able to trust and listen.
- Established and profitable with the means to invest in your future.
- 100% committed to creating and executing *your* plan for affluent prosperity.

...then this book is for you.

In this book, I share ways to help you achieve more with less. Some of what I suggest may seem obvious, but ask yourself the question: "Am I actually doing it?" If you're reading this book, I'm willing to bet you're not—and therein lies the problem.

There are many reasons people don't do what they know they should be doing. Time and accountability are two big ones.

You don't have enough time to change because you're too busy working in the business. Your accountability is to deliver value for your clients. Right? You feel the pressure every day to make sure your clients get what they want, when they want it, at the price they want to pay. Sound familiar?

Guess what? You're not running your business; your clients are. I'll show you how to change this, how to put you back in charge of your business, and how to attract the right clients at the right prices so you are more profitable for less work. More profit for less work leads to personal sovereignty and affluent prosperity.

And that means putting rules in place for your business, your clients, and most of all, for you.

I like to write with stories, and I'll illustrate my business rules with stories of how business owners I know progress from discomfort to sovereignty and ultimately to affluent prosperity. I draw some stories from my own experiences, and some are experiences I've gathered from clients. They are all true.

You too can achieve sustainable wealth, a richer lifestyle, and an enduring legacy with less financial hassle.

Are You Ready to Start?

I've said before that I run my business not just to earn a living but because I love seeing my clients thrive. This book is aimed at business owners because I'm a business owner myself, and I've benefited from the support of other business owners for many years. I know how important support and accountability is if we want to stop struggling, start growing, and turn our businesses into profit-making machines. If this book gives you just one idea that makes a positive difference to you, then I will be delighted.

Why do I talk about business owners and not "normal" people, people with jobs and worries just like any other? Because business owners tend to be entrepreneurial, which means they take risks, can be more open-minded and flexible, and are often more willing to try new things. It's a massive generalisation, of course, but entrepreneurs do tend to have a different mindset.

I want personal sovereignty: control of my day, my future, and my work, and that comes from working with people who are flexible, driven, and committed to *their* financial future.

Maybe you're ready to take a step towards personal sovereignty and affluent prosperity right now, and that's brilliant.

Maybe you're not quite ready yet, and that's okay too. This book will help you get prepared for the day when you're ready to embrace change.

In it, I'll talk about general mindset, wealth mindset, and business mindset; control, other people's opinions, pricing, and value. I'll start you on the road to personal sovereignty and affluent prosperity, show you a perspective you may not have encountered before, and nudge you into gear.

But only you can choose to press the accelerator or keep your foot on the brake.

What will it be? Are you ready to dive into your next big adventure—or are you comfortable where you are?

1

KNOW YOUR ENEMY

THE FIRST PLACE SUCCESS HAPPENS IS INSIDE YOUR HEAD

A s you turn into land, the low fuel lights are likely to flicker on and off as the aircraft banks."

As we approached the ship, the low fuel lights did exactly that, indicating roughly five to ten minutes of fuel remaining. Our instructor in the back told us a story of a student crew returning from a night sortie like this one a few years earlier. As their aircraft banked into land, the flickering low fuel lights distracted the pilot. They crashed into the sea, killing both onboard. A timely reminder of how dangerous our job could be.

The only reason we had a ship to land on was because it had to turn around to pick us up. It wasn't just flickering lights as we banked; we were, in fact, low on fuel.

How embarrassing.

Running out of fuel is the cardinal sin for aircrew, short of actually crashing.

This was my final check flight, my very last flight in my Royal Navy flying training, then I was free and onto the front lines. I was excited—and I was pissed off, too.

The night before, I just wanted a solid night's rest, but I was wound tighter than an alternator coil. We were somewhere in the Bay of Biscay, in February, heading roughly north with a heavy sea coming in on the port side. This meant the ship was rolling, a lot. It's hard to sleep when you're shifting in your bunk all night. I was frustrated—angry with the weather, the ship, the time of year.

You name it, I was annoyed with it.

I'd slept perfectly well through many rough nights before, but tonight felt different because of how much was riding on my final check flight the next day. Instead of letting go of all the factors I couldn't control, I got more and more angry and frustrated.

Guess what happened?

My final check flight the next evening was terrible. So terrible, I nearly ran out of fuel. It was made worse because the Squadron Commanding Officer was in the back of the helicopter assessing me. This wasn't especially unusual, because he'd seen how well I was doing and wanted the pleasure of shaking my hand on landing. (So he told me some years later.)

In my haste to prioritise dealing with the "enemy" (a successful missile strike on an enemy frigate at 100 feet at night over heavy seas), I failed to prioritise self-preservation. I failed to ensure the survival of the aircraft and crew to fight another day—and it was entirely my own fault.

I should have recognised my judgement was sleep-impaired and postponed the flight. This was only training; safety did not need to be compromised. But by that stage of training, all I wanted was one percent above the pass mark so I could get on the front line.

Instead, I nearly ran out of fuel and had to ask the ship to turn around and fetch us or we'd have been going for a swim. Not my finest hour, given how well I had done in flying training until that point.

Of course, I blamed everything but myself at the time.

Needless to say, we landed safely, and the debrief was long

and detailed. I learned the most valuable lesson of my career, which I will touch on throughout this book.

The lesson was not, "Don't run out of fuel."

The lesson was this: if we focus on the result (a pass and getting onto the front line) to the detriment of the process (staying safe), we put our very survival at risk.

It took me years before I grew up and stopped blaming the weather.

"Know your enemy" is an old military adage, and it's very relevant to you and your business. The list of enemies we see as conspiring to stop us achieving our very best is long and distinguished: clients, family, markets, industry, competitors, parents, money, social media, friends, press, economy, politicians, HMRC...

Before you read on, stop and consider how many of those you see as barriers, hurdles, and problems within your business? Do you believe they're preventing you from achieving the greatness you deserve? Do you feel frustrated that you're not achieving the results you want? Frustrated that other people don't see your value as you do?

If so, I have splendid news for you. The above list is complete and utter rubbish. This list of enemies is only true if you accept it to be true.

The frustration you feel is very common for business owners. It stems from not being able to control things that are important to your business, like results. Like other people's actions (for example, clients who mess about or push for discounts).

I've been there. Frustrated with factors outside my control.

I was there in the Bay of Biscay, that February, on my last flight in Royal Navy flying training.

If only I'd been able to let go of that frustration and take ownership of my actions.

Take Ownership of Blame

Once upon a time, my natural response to adversity or to things going wrong was to blame external factors. Like when I blamed everything under the sun for my terrible final check flight performance. Is that your natural response, too?

It's okay if it is. It's normal to react like this; most people do. We're conditioned to. But remember: you are not normal. You are an exceptional human being. You are an individual, not part of a hive mind (like the Borg[1]). You are a business owner, passionate about what you do, compelled to deliver fantastic quality and value.

You are in charge of your thinking. You have a choice: to accept blame as truth, or stick two fingers up to blame and take back control.

This can be quite challenging because we're bombarded with negative messages day in, day out. They're everywhere, because bad news sells. We lap it up. We listen to it. We even start to believe it. This is brainwashing, pure and simple. We're conditioned to accept the world as a terrible place full of suffering and war, with economic disaster looming around every corner. Much of what we see in the media is death, destruction, terrorism, homelessness, bankruptcy, murder, knife crime. Because we're conditioned to it, we expect it— which reinforces our negative beliefs.

These constant messages reinforce our subconscious stories and negative inner voice. A voice that says things like, "I could, but it isn't the right time." Or, "I can't put my prices up when the economy is so weak." Or, "It's not the right weather." And so on. We all have these ingrained stories about ourselves and our lives, and when we hear a story often enough, we start to believe it.

The truth is, we have the power to change our inner stories—and thus change our lives.

I recall sitting with a new client some years ago whose

internal story was very negative. His whole demeanour, his thoughts, beliefs, and actions, all supported the result he was getting.

Now, we can argue about how he arrived in this place, but the facts were clear: he was earning plenty, but kept racking up uncontrollable high-interest credit card debt. He didn't have a retirement plan, and his entire conversation around money was negative. He thought he was stuck in a debt spiral.

He believed this is simply how things were, so he carried on taking the same old actions. Lo! and behold, my client ended up with the same result every time: more debt and more stress.

This result reinforced his belief that he couldn't do anything about it. His beliefs became a self-fulfilling prophecy, and he remained stuck in a vicious circle.

This cycle of Thoughts > Beliefs > Actions > Results stemmed from one place: his thoughts. If you change your thoughts, which will alter your beliefs (about yourself, your clients, and your business), your actions will change, and you will get different results. The secret is to change your thoughts so you ultimately create positive results.

I showed this client how to improve his situation, get his debt under control, and start saving for retirement. Given he was 59, this was extremely important to him. Slowly, his thoughts showed a more positive outlook. He started to believe life could be different, his actions changed, and now he has the result he was looking for—financial peace of mind and a retirement plan that makes sense for him.

Kumbaya

It's easy to slip back into old habits, though. Changing the way we think is a learned skill and we have to keep practising. Hence the value of good mentoring and being held accountable for our thoughts, beliefs, and actions. Constant support and reminders help us become more self-aware, and banish negativity to the back seat where it belongs.

I call the negative part of my brain Mikey. He's a mischievous monkey, prone to dancing around. He's unfocused, confused, and negative: think Gollum/Sméagol in *The Lord of the Rings*. If Mikey is your natural state, you're probably telling yourself negative stories grounded in the experience of your early years.

Mikey surfaced for me when I was six or seven years old at a school concert. I don't recall the exact song my class was singing—perhaps it was *Kumbaya*—but the boys were dressed as cowboys and I was holding a mini-guitar-type-thing, pretending to strum. I was having a great time singing my heart out until the teacher told me to mime for the concert because my singing voice was so out of tune. That one minor event triggered a complete lack of confidence in anything remotely musical.

The funny thing is, I ended up being schooled at a specialist music school—and I'm tone deaf, so it caused me no end of paradoxical amusement.

To this day, nothing on earth will possess me to sing in front of anyone. That lack of confidence is still with me, even in the middle of a friend's church wedding when I'm drowned out by better singers. However, I have stopped caring that my singing is terrible, which it is by the way. I mean, it sounds lovely to me in the shower, but apparently I warble in an amusingly bad way. Ah well, it sounds good to me and I feel good singing it, which is all that matters.

(I'll still mumble into the hymn book at weddings, though; that'll never change.)

Do you have similar memories? Are there events in your early life that shaped your attitudes and beliefs today?

It goes deeper than this, even though I know and understand what is happening in my mind, because we spend much of our lives being appraised. Feedback is a fundamental part of schooling and further education. What's most interesting about it is this: we are actively encouraged to put more effort into stuff we're not very good at and don't enjoy. This sets the tone for the rest of our lives. If we're not very good at something, work harder at it—regardless of whether or not we *want* to become good at it.

Ever had an appraisal which focused on areas you could improve? Or client feedback that you're disorganised or didn't reply fast enough or (insert any other negative or constructive feedback)?

What did you do with that information?

Did you put all your energy into improving something you're not very good at? Did you focus on negative traits? Did you let Mikey out of the cage to whisper negative thoughts into your ear?

It's far better to be excellent at a few things you enjoy than to spend time and energy improving things you don't enjoy. At best, the gains you'll get will be miniscule. It makes much more sense to hire specialists for the stuff that's not your forte and work hard to excel where you're already good.

This was my experience at school in English Literature classes. I didn't see the point in dissecting the author's thinking about a particular chapter or paragraph.

Firstly, why not just ask the author what they were thinking instead of trying to second guess what they might have been thinking (which to my mind is projection and using my imagination and therefore utterly pointless)?

Secondly, I really didn't give a damn, anyway. A book, as far as I was concerned, was an interesting diversion for the mind away from reality. Escapism into a different world. I had absolutely no interest in dissecting *To Kill a Mockingbird* week after bloody week. I hated critique with a passion. That's probably why I'm surprised to find myself writing a book. Funny how things change.

Working hard to improve our skills is vital—as long as it's

in an area we want to improve and which will serve us. The reason I struggled so much in English Literature was because I had no interest in pursuing a career in dissecting literature; I just wanted to read for fun.

Make Friends with Indifference

I want you to become indifferent to other people's opinions.

This may seem controversial and most people will naturally baulk at it because we are conditioned to care what other people think—or, more correctly, what we *think* they think. The reality is, we have a choice because most of us get to choose what we think about. We can *choose* to give all our attention to other people's unqualified opinions… or we can *choose* to ignore them. We can *choose* to be indifferent to what other people may or may not think about us. And we *choose* whether to react to it.

The best examples of unqualified opinions come from social media. Think about the number of people offering up their strongly held opinion as fact on any topic you choose to name. Like Karen or Trev down the road, who are expert epidemiologists and opine with utter conviction that COVID-19 is "just flu". Or Donald Trump and pretty much everything that comes out of his mouth. The simple fact is, people with extreme and opinionated views tend to be people who know the least about a topic.[2]

So what we often see on social media is unsolicited negative feedback from a completely unknown person in a completely different field of work telling you how to run your business. They're the funniest ones: the airline pilot offering their strongly held opinion that you would find more clients if you didn't swear so much on social media. People who swear will be attracted to people who swear.

This goes for potential customers, too. You might be inclined to worry if a potential customer says something like,

"Your prices are too high." Or, "You need to do this differently for me to buy from you."

They're absolutely entitled to their opinion, but they're not entitled to make you listen or act on it.

My point is this: choose carefully who you listen to. For every person who doesn't like something you say or the way you do things, there'll be another person who loves it. You cannot be everything to everybody, and if you try, you'll make yourself miserable.

Imagine what would happen if you ran your business trying desperately to please all the negative doom-mongers in your potential client base. You might, if you're lucky, make them slightly happy. But if they're negative people, constantly looking to drive you down on price, service and value, they'll probably never be happy.

However, you've put time and energy (and probably money) into cultivating these negative people and you now have clients who are difficult to work with, who are rarely happy with what you do, who don't value your work, and who push you down on price. You've modified your business and your behaviour to please clients you don't want to work with.

It gets worse, though. By creating a business that caters to difficult clients, you have created a business that is attractive to difficult clients, because you bend over backwards to do exactly what they ask.

Why would you do that? Why would you deliberately attract the type of clients you don't want to work with?

You do it because you're afraid. You do it because of Mikey. You do it because you care too much about the unqualified opinions of people who are not involved in running your business. You can listen to suggestions (and some of them will be good)—but honestly, your clients (and family and friends) do not know best. It is your business. Only you know what's best for you, your family, and your business.

So, if you're not happy with the clients you have, let them go. Fire them. It's very cathartic.

That all sounds pretty scary, right? So consider this scenario instead. You are confident in your ability to do what you do best. You're an expert in what you do, and you do it very well. You don't need to listen to people who have never run a business or who don't work in your industry. Position yourself as such: set out what you do, why you do it, and how you work—and then offer your services to those who want to work with you.

That level of confidence in business will mean you get far fewer unsolicited and unqualified opinions, and you'll attract the people who want to work with an expert. People who want to put their problem into your hands so you can solve it for them. People who trust you to do what you do best and are happy to pay you well for your expertise.

Hire for Your Weaknesses

If you're not good at something, hire someone who is, instead of wasting time and energy trying to get better at things you're not good at and don't enjoy. Richard Branson describes this is one of the smartest things any business owner can and should do: hire for your weaknesses. Instead, most business owners tend to hire people like themselves, because it feels comfortable to do so. Or, we try to do it all ourselves—and fail miserably. It takes courage to admit we're not good at something in our business and ask someone else to do it for us.

If we hire people just like ourselves, though, we build a business of clones. We need diversity; we need unique skills and outlooks, and we need to delegate the stuff we're not good at (or hate doing) to someone who is good at it (and loves doing it).

If you hate bookkeeping, hire a bookkeeper. (In fact, hire a bookkeeper and accountant anyway, we should not be doing our own accounts.)

Hate fixing laptops? Hire an IT guru (or buy a Mac!)

Hate client follow up? Hire a smiley, friendly, outgoing person who loves talking to clients.

Hate having to think about your financial future and don't know where to start? Hire a financial expert.

This might sound like a big investment and you might think you can't afford it, but I guarantee that if you make this investment in yourself and your business, it will pay off in both profits and happiness.

You don't have to hire everyone all at once; start small. If you do your own accounts now and it takes hours and hours of frustration, find a great accountant. This is the perfect place to start outsourcing because an excellent accountant will save you far more than they cost you.

Then you move onto the next thing you'd rather not do yourself and invest the savings.

When you free up your time to focus on what you're best at, you'll be able to improve your own focus and business productivity, raise your prices, attract higher-paying clients, and your business will grow.

There is absolutely no point doing stuff you hate or aren't good at. If you want to achieve personal sovereignty and affluent prosperity, you must be ruthlessly efficient with your time and money. Sustainable wealth, a richer lifestyle, and an enduring legacy is achievable, but only you can make it so.

It's easy to make excuses. It's easy to believe no-one else does it properly; just because it's not the way you'd do it, doesn't mean it's wrong. Wrong just means different.

It's easy to say a job only takes you two hours a week, so you can do it yourself… but what could you do with those two hours a week? That's eight hours a month. Which is a whopping 96 hours—or four days—a year.

When you look at it like that—gifting yourself an extra

four days a year—isn't it worth *finding* time to hire someone? And if you're worried you can't afford it, use the time you save to put your prices up and find higher-paying clients to cover the investment.

If your business is profitable and you have the means to invest in your future, which should be the case if you're reading this book, start by investing in someone to deal with the stuff you hate and get it off your plate.

Excuses are natural, particularly when they're of the "no one else does it properly" variety. We business owners tend to be control freaks and letting go is hard to do, but we need to do it if we are to succeed.

If your natural reaction is to make an excuse, this next section is for you.

Blame, Shame, Judgement, and Criticism

We all have choices. We can choose to blame, shame, judge, and criticise. Or we can choose to take personal responsibility for what goes on in our lives.

I'm a big fan of the 80/20 principle, which states that 80% of outcomes come from 20% of causes (more or less).

For most people—80% of them—their world revolves around blame, shame, judgement, and criticism. Donald Trump is a marvellous example: have you ever seen him take personal responsibility for something? Not a chance. Ever seen him blaming someone else? Ever seen him deriding and putting other people down? All the time. That's called shame. He has deep-rooted self-esteem issues and a colossal ego. He is his own worst enemy, if only he would open his eyes and see.

It's clear that you can achieve enormous wealth and superficial success through bullying, bluff, and bravado to massage your own ego. You can spend your life angry and irritated with people. You can lie, cheat, and bully your way to wealth. But those people will never be happy because they have yet to learn to love themselves.

It doesn't feel good to trample over everybody to get what you want. It doesn't feel good to shame, blame, judge, and criticise so you can feel better about yourself (except you won't actually feel any better). Until you learn to love and accept yourself for who you are, you will never be truly happy.

What's interesting about this type of narcissist is they're never happy. They go through life lashing out, quick-tempered and mean-spirited, with the single goal to accumulate wealth and possessions. I don't know about you, but I want to avoid these types of people.

If you're being painfully honest with yourself, perhaps you sometimes exhibit some of these behaviours. That's okay: welcome to the club. I've been there, done that, and still do it on occasion. None of us is perfect.

Recognising our weaknesses is the first step to becoming a better person—and running a great business.

The real problem with blame, shame, judgement, and criticism is the negative mindset that comes with it. If we're not taking personal responsibility, then we're already in a negative mindset spiral. A few people will bully their way out of it, but most will blame everyone and everything else for their lack of success.

The truth is, only one person is responsible for our success (or lack of it). That person looks back at us from the mirror every day.

If we *choose* to spend our time thinking negative thoughts, we will continue to experience the world as we *choose* to think it is.

"As you think, so shall you become."

If you think you're going to have a bad day, you will. Guaranteed.

If you think your business will only ever be mediocre, it will. Guaranteed.

If, on the other hand, you choose to think (and believe) you *can* do it, you're much more likely to. Not guaranteed; but you'll give yourself a flying start.

It's entirely up to you.

So, let's get started.

What's Next?

The advice "know your enemy" is good advice—but only if we're honest about who our enemy really is.

Most successful business owners understand they are both the weakest link in their business and the foundation of it. They work on growing and improving themselves at least as much as they work on and in the business.

Here are three simple things you can practice:

1. Keep a journal: note down all negative thoughts that pop into your head. When did they happen? Why? What was the trigger? How did you react and how did you *feel?* When we become aware of our reactions, we can change them and notice what we have control over.

2. Practise being indifferent to the unqualified and unsolicited opinions of others. Brené Brown suggests taking a small piece of paper and writing on it the names of the people whose opinions matter to you. When you get negative feedback or criticism, check your piece of paper. Did it come from one of those people? If not, perhaps you can ignore it.

3. Get to know and understand blame, shame, judgement, and criticism. I recommend reading Brené Brown's books *The Power of Vulnerability* and *The Gifts of Imperfection,* and listening to her podcast *Unlocking Us.*

2

MONEY MINDSET
WHAT DOES "RICH" MEAN TO YOU?

In the film *Titanic*, there's a scene where the rich guy tries to pay for a place in the lifeboat. The officer in the lifeboat says, "Your money can't save you anymore than it can save me."

There's a lesson there for all of us, rich or poor: money is only worth the value it adds to your life. Buying a new Ferrari and flaunting monetary wealth does not necessarily add value to your life.

I often wonder what's behind ostentatious displays of wealth and status when I hear people in the pub comparing the size of their... jet-skis, speedboats, cars, and properties. Don't get me wrong: I understand these things can be fun, and I'm not knocking the way people enjoy their money.

I just don't understand bragging about it.

I prefer to talk about my family, how I'm feeling about my life, and the stuff we do together, like splashing in the stream in the woods with the dog and kids.

I get why haring around the warm Mediterranean on a jet-ski would be fun, but it's short-lived adrenalin which, much like drug taking, requires constant topping up followed by the next bigger, faster, more expensive rush.

I guess we just have a different outlook and different values, and that's fine by me. I prefer the Stoic idea of living a good life: when I'm on my deathbed, will I be proud of the stuff I own, or the people I've helped?

How about you?

Money is fun, and spending it on fun stuff is great… But being present in the moment with the people who bring you the greatest joy and love, your family, never gets boring or wears thin. And you don't need oodles of money to do that.

"How much is an oodle, Daddy?"

One of my children once asked me, "How much money is there, Daddy?" It's an interesting question because we have to start by asking what money is. Money is just a store of value. We exchange it for something of value to us, which the recipient can then use to exchange for something of value to them.

In physical terms, money is notes and coins in people's pockets plus their bank balances. In economic terms, the closest measure is called M4 or Broad Money. I'm not going into detail as it gets over-complicated and I don't want you to fall asleep!

To answer my child's question, I looked up M4 and told him it was about £2.75 trillion in the UK.

That's rather a lot of money.

And what about this quantitative easing thing, or QE? It's been around for more than a decade because of the 2008 financial crisis. QE basically means the Bank of England prints more money. They don't actually print physical bank notes, though. The Bank opens a bank account for itself, adds some electronic money to it, then buys government bonds and corporate debt; the Bank is effectively lending new money to other Banks and large businesses to fund investment.

This has the effect of increasing the amount of money the

government and banks (who loaned the money to the corporations) have available to spend. Thus, the Bank has increased the amount of money the government can spend to build roads, for example (which keeps people in jobs) and the amount banks can spend through lending it to businesses and individuals.

If banks, businesses, and people stop spending, we head into recession—so it's important that spending continues.

If people feel wealthy, they'll spend. If they feel poor, they won't spend—which is bad for business and ultimately bad for the people who've stopped spending. It's all about confidence. You'll hear the term consumer confidence bandied around in the newspapers and on the news if you watch it.

Consumer confidence is a big part of what drives economic policy because policymakers want people to feel confident. To feel good. To spend. Because spending drives growth and increases GDP and creates a feel-good economy. It's a more more more attitude which is more about re-election than long-term sustainability.

Somehow, we need to transition our economy away from growth as the only measure of our success, to one of sustainability. We can't just keep building stuff ad infinitum. One day, we just need to stop and be happy with what we have.

And that's what your money story is all about. Knowing when enough is enough.

I know I espouse sustainable wealth, richer lifestyle, and an enduring legacy, but let's be clear—that's not at any cost. What I'm advocating is achieving a position of personal sovereignty and affluent prosperity, where you have the time and money to do the things you want to do. I want you to have choices.

I want you to have enough of what you need to bask in happiness and the richness of wealth (by which I mean far more than just money) instead of constantly striving for the next white elephant. It's about balance: the balance between working every hour possible to fund an expensive material lifestyle and having enough that you can truly enjoy soaking up the smell of rain on a damp woodland floor.

I know exactly where I would rather be. What about you?

This isn't about judging you for the choices you make; it's about helping you create a life that allows you to enjoy your choices. It comes down to whether you seek achievement or fulfilment.

Your Money Story

When I look back at my early experiences in the Royal Navy, I see a young man who just wanted to serve and fly. It was never for the money, which was a good thing because the money was pretty pants given the risks we took. In fact, how much money I made never really crossed my mind.

I remember having a conversation in the pub with a former naval aviator a decade or more after leaving the Navy. We had been crewed together for the final stages of operational flying training, and later onboard HMS York, so we knew each other well. We both left the Navy at about the same time, for different reasons, and we both entered the corporate world.

We were reminiscing about our service and reflecting on the path our lives had taken.

I had just quit the corporate rat race, and he was CEO for the UK brand of a multinational. We were talking about why we joined the Navy and how the financial reward was completely irrelevant because we believed in what we were doing and loved every minute.

Our money story was about service and internal wealth, not cash.

In our corporate lives, though, we were both caught up in the accumulation of money and wealth, but neither of us were truly happy with it. We weren't fulfilling our innate need to help and serve that drove us to join the military.

We weren't helping anyone in corporate land, not really. We weren't directly doing good. We were prostituting our leadership and management skills for cash, and we had lost sight of our core values. That's partly why I quit the corporate world to run my own business. It's why my friend also quit his multi-national role.

We realised that, for us, wealth and success were about far more than just money.

What's your current story? Are you caught up in an accumulation race that isn't you? Do you feel under pressure to brag about your jet-ski or the size of the television you've just bought? Do you find yourself wondering why you're doing all this? (That's shame feelings, by the way.)

Are you in charge of creating your money story, or is it creating you? Are you really in control of your money story? What does wealth and being rich mean to you?

You may assume it means money, and that's part of it, for sure, but it's not the essence of my why. For me, wealth and feeling rich is about the personal sovereignty I mentioned earlier.

It's about having enough money and enough time to enjoy my freedom. Not endlessly more, but enough. Enough to know I can spend more time with my kids and not worry about paying the mortgage. Enough to know I can work four days a week so my wife and I can spend a day together. Enough to know I am happy and in control of my destiny.

I choose to ensure my story isn't being written by the fiscal demands upon me. I am writing my money story from my thoughts, beliefs, and actions.

This is because our attitude to money, and understanding of it, affects our future prosperity. Much like our business mindset has a profound effect on the success of our business, our money mindset affects our wealth. If we think we're worth

X, we'll *believe* we're worth X, so we behave in ways that lead us to create X. For example, if you think you could only ever earn £20k, or £40k, or £100k... that's what will happen. You'll limit yourself.

As you say it, so it shall become.

Imagine keeping a diary of your thoughts and feelings about money, and how much actual money you have, every day. The diary is your money story; a story about your attitude to money and how that attitude plays out in your real life. Your future money story will be grounded in your past money story. Are you consciously writing your future money story, or has it already been written by your past? In other words, you get to decide how your money story plays out through your thoughts, beliefs, and actions.

Is your past money story limiting your future prosperity? Are you being held back by limiting beliefs? If so, only you can change things.

Mahatma Gandhi said our beliefs become our thoughts, our thoughts become our words, our words become our actions, our actions become our habits, our habits become our values, and our values become our destiny.

What we think and believe will determine our destiny.

Negative Money Beliefs

If you're going to change your money story, it starts with you. You write your own story so only you can change it. Look at the list of statements below. How many of them do you believe or can you relate to?

- It takes money to make money
- Money is the root of all evil
- Rich people are greedy
- It's better to be poor and happy than rich and sad
- Money can't buy happiness

- I've never had money
- Rich people are just lucky
- I've left it too late to save for retirement
- I don't know how much I owe
- I don't make enough money to save anything

I could write an almost endless list of negative money thoughts. If you have a negative thought about money, negativity is exactly what will happen. You need to change your thinking and beliefs to change your actions and results. Sounds easy, doesn't it? It isn't.

It isn't easy because the habit is already formed. Our story has already been written, and the belief is entrenched in our neural pathways, in the way we think. It takes effort and commitment to change. That can only come from you, by changing your thoughts and beliefs.

How Nick, how?

I'm no psychologist, but I do know this: if you want to run a marathon, you have to train for it. You start with short runs and you build up. You take rest days and gym days. You gradually improve strength and endurance until you can run 26.2 miles.

It's the same with thoughts and beliefs. There isn't a magic pill to take; we have to work at it. We have to recognise when the story we're telling ourselves is negative and not serving us well. The first step is recognition. Then we need to consciously think a different thought. It feels alien at first, but as we practice, it gets easier—until it becomes second nature.

Writing this book is a great example. When I first considered doing it, I thought, "How the hell am I going to do that? I haven't got time, I don't know where to start, I'm not sure I have the skills. Why would people read it? It'll be boring."

They were all negative thoughts.

It took considerable willpower to retrain my thoughts and a good dose of pig-headed self-belief to turn that around.

It also took support. Some things you just can't do on your own. I turned to Vicky Quinn Fraser of Moxie Books, who was invaluable in helping me structure and plan this book. I still had to write it, mind—there was no outsourcing here. But she kept me positive and focused. She helped me eradicate negative thoughts and believe that I could do it.

It's the same with your money story. Eradicate negative thoughts, stay focused on positive outcomes, and put the right support structure in place. But we can't know everything, which is why getting expert financial support and advice is so important.

When I arrived at 702 Squadron for my Lynx helicopter flying training, it was all completely new. I didn't know how to operate the aircraft. I didn't know how the radar and the other systems worked. I knew nothing.

I could have said to myself, "I'll never learn all this," or "I'm not good enough to make it," which are all negative thoughts. Or I could just get stuck into the books and start learning. Like the marathon training, like writing a book, it takes time and starts with a small step.

Training our minds works exactly the same way.

I didn't suddenly know what to do in the event of a double engine failure; I had to learn it. I had to practice in the simulator. I had to understand how the aircraft behaves, what the systems do, and what it all means. That all took time and it sometimes felt frustrating. But as each day went by, I got better and better. It was damn hard work, the hardest thing I've ever done by a long shot. Flying training was draining and utterly demanding of my focus and attention.

When it comes to your money story, you need to recognise when it's not serving you well and take action to change it. If you believe any of the statements I listed earlier, then you need to find a new mantra to replace the negative, unhelpful thought. For example, you could replace "it takes money to make money" with "I am good at what I do, I add value to people's lives, and they are happy to pay me for my help and expertise." Or you could replace "I don't earn enough to save for retirement" with, "I'm going to save £30 next week by not going out on Friday night."

Note that I haven't used the word 'try.' As Yoda said, "Do or do not. There is no try." If you answer your negative money thoughts with a non-committal "try" to change, it'll not happen because you're not fully committed. With the word try, you're giving yourself a mental get-out clause. You know it's true; how many times have you said you'll "try" to attend an event you don't really want to go to... then somehow failed to make it?

When we use the word "try", we've already decided to fail. If you're going to change, you need to fully commit with no get-out clause.

Sure, you might have some failures along the way; get used to it. If you're in business, you're going to have failures—and that's perfectly normal. It's good, in fact. I talk more about this in chapter 5: Discomfort and Grit.

"But I wanna be rich!"

If your primary thought is you want to be rich, you're going about things the wrong way. You're defining success in terms of material things, rather than in terms of freedom. Being rich isn't about oodles of money, it's about choice—and that means different things to different people.

If personal sovereignty and affluent prosperity is your goal, rather than simply increasing the numbers in your bank account, then this book and the work I do will absolutely help you.

Richness comes from the value we add to people's lives. If you have a good idea, a solid work ethic, and you believe in yourself, then you will attract investment in your business. If the product or service you offer is valuable to people, they will pay you for it.

A good idea doesn't have to be something completely new, untried, and innovative. Thousands of people start businesses that solve the same problems other businesses already solve, and they make good money doing it. The reality is, you're probably not going to be the next Mark Zuckerberg—and why would you want to be, anyway? If you truly believe in what you do and what you offer is valuable, then you will have richness in your life, however you define it.

With richness comes choices. When you start to make money from the value you add for your clients, you'll want to do something with your money to enhance your personal sovereignty and achieve affluent prosperity. What holds most people back is the following thought: "But I don't understand investing, it's so confusing. Why bother?"

I get it. Investment can be confusing. But you have a choice. You can wallow in confusion and ignore the opportunity, or you can do something about it.

As Yoda said, "Do or do not. There is no try."

So, let's do.

What's Next?

Let's start with your money story. You can allow your experiences and beliefs to dictate your future wealth (or lack thereof)—or you can write a new money story, starting today.

As C. S. Lewis said, "You can't go back and change the beginning, but you can start where you are and change the ending."

Here are three simple things you can do right now:

1. Every time you have a negative thought about money, wealth, or "rich people", write it down—

then consider why you feel that way. Turn the negative thought into a positive one. For example, if I saw someone had just bought their dream house, and my initial reaction was one of bitterness: "Flash bastard!" I'd turn it into glad thoughts: "Good for him. He's worked hard and earned it."

2. Remember, money is just a tool; nothing more. When you think of it like that, what could you do with it? For yourself, your family, for fun, or to make the world a better place?

3. Decide what being wealthy or rich means to you. It's not always about money. One of the key aspects of the work I do is setting out your life plan, so consider writing a life plan: what would your ideal day, week, month, year look like? Where do you want to be in a year, five years, ten years?

3

THOUGHTS, BELIEFS, AND ACTIONS

THE STORIES WE TELL OURSELVES AND HOW THEY RUN OUR LIVES

For years I suffered with hay fever. Throughout my childhood and twenties, I kept going to my GP who kept offering me the same tired old drugs which didn't work. They just made me fall asleep or go doo-lally.

I'd fall asleep constantly throughout the day and it was embarrassing.

We'd be out with friends at a National Trust property, and I'd steal a couple of 30-minute naps on an uncomfortable park bench. My one-hour commute would take two hours because I'd have to make two stops for 30-minute sleeps.

My head was constantly fuzzy, and I was totally un-alert.

In my thirties, I stopped taking any medication as it didn't help at all. I believed that nothing could improve my hay fever. The result of my actions—in this case, stopping medical treatment and seeing no improvement in my symptoms—reinforced my belief that nothing could help me. When my then-girlfriend suggested a new treatment, my immediate reaction was, "That won't work!" because that was my belief. My past experience told me that nothing could help.

I was re-affirming a deeply held belief in my mind, and that belief controlled my action (or inaction, in this case).

So, I did nothing, again, and re-affirmed the belief that nothing works.

Confirmation Bias

In Chapters 1 and 2, I mentioned the importance of thoughts, beliefs, and actions. They are central to our ability to focus on what's important and within our control.

Our thoughts drive our beliefs.

If we think something doesn't work, and we think it often enough, we come to believe it doesn't work.

As you say it (think it), so it shall become (result).

Beliefs drive our actions.

We may think we're not very good at writing, so our self-talk says we can't possibly write a book (belief), so we don't write (we take no action). Taking no action is in itself a decision.

The result is we don't write a book. We review the result—still no book—and think "See, I can't possibly write a book because I haven't written a book." This is confirmation bias—our tendency to search for and remember information that confirms our existing beliefs. We've told ourselves we can't do something—and lo! and behold, that's exactly what we find.

As you say it, so it shall become.

If we instead think there might be something else we can do, if we allow ourselves to believe something else might work, we will take a different action, and may end up with a different—better—result.

Our thoughts drive our beliefs.

Our beliefs drive our actions.

Our actions create results.

If you keep doing the same actions, you will get the same results.

To take different actions, requires different thoughts and beliefs.

If you take different actions, you will get different results.

Kaizen: Process vs Outcome

This chain of thoughts, beliefs, and actions is a process. It is a controllable process that we, the business owner, can change, adapt, and adjust at will. The result we get from our actions is the outcome of the process.

Given that we have no control of results because we have no control over a client's decision to buy (or not), there's no point focusing on results. This is why it's crucial to focus on the process—our thoughts, beliefs, and actions—and not the result.

Of course the result is important—after all, we're running our businesses for a reason—but our results *only* reflect the effectiveness of our thoughts, beliefs, and actions.

The result (which we can't control) is the outcome of our process (which we can control).

So, we need to focus on building the process, focus on what we can control, and use the results of the process to improve the actions we take. See what works and make it better. Abandon or refine what doesn't work. Test, and test again.

Instead of becoming frustrated with poor results, we can put our energy elsewhere and channel our frustration into refining and testing the process, using the results as the measure of process success.

This idea of testing and measuring is crucial and I'll come back to it in more detail later in this book. For now, though, it's enough to know our numbers, so we can measure the results of the actions we're taking. There's no point taking action if we don't know how effective it is.

In marketing, for example, we do this via A/B testing. Let's say we're sending sales emails: 50% of the emails would have one subject line, and 50% would use a different subject line, to test which one works best. Next time, we take the winning email and split test it again—perhaps this time testing the first paragraph, or the call to action, or the offer. And so on and so on.

The aim is to continually refine the process, so it gets better and better.

In Japan, they call this Kaizen, or continuous improvement.

The best way to do this is to put systems in place to measure the results of our process.

So, we've established that the process drives results, and this starts with our thoughts. But what drives thoughts?

If we ignore other people's actions and opinions, our thoughts stem from our core values—like love and connection, integrity, and honesty. Most people give little conscious thought to their values, accepting them as part of who they are. But what are your values? What are the values that describe who you are and why you do what you do? The values that drive your thoughts and ultimately create results?

People who value doing the right thing think about doing the right thing. People who value cheating or taking short cuts think about taking those actions. Our values are at the core of what drives us and our businesses.

I spent some time with a coach who helped me understand my core values, because sometimes we can't see the wood for the trees.

My values were real in the sense that they've always been there, driving my thoughts, beliefs, and actions. I'd just never written them down or given any conscious thought to what they were. The values that came out of the work I did with my coach drive my thinking, and my business actions, and ultimately my results.

My values are central to what I do, and why I do it. I'll share my values below:

- Freedom
- Courage
- Confidence
- Integrity
- Health (mental and physical)
- Love and affection
- Connection
- Fun

These are all relevant to my business. Now, I'm not saying I want to fall in love with all my clients (or vice versa), but I do want to love what I do, which is handy as I have a genuine passion to help people.

These are the values at the heart of my thoughts. My values and my rules give structure to my thoughts and beliefs, and they drive my actions, which create the results in my business. More on rules in Chapter 7.

Your values and your rules define why you do what you do.

Simon Sinek talks a lot about our why and how important it is. "People don't buy what you do; they buy why you do it. What you do simply proves what you believe."

People don't buy make-up. They buy confidence.

People don't buy houses. They buy lifestyles and safe places.

People don't buy condoms. They buy peace of mind.

The experience of buying a product or service, or more accurately the experience you are buying, is often more important than the function the product or service provides. The same is true of *your* business. The client's experience stems from your business values and rules, and it is this experience—the outcome and the way the outcome makes them *feel*—that they are really purchasing, not the product itself.

What's Next?

The key to changing our results is to look at the actions we're taking—and what's driving our actions. This stems from our values.

1. Reflect on your core values. What's really important to you and why?
2. Google "personal values list". Without giving it too much thought, put a tick by each value that resonates with you. Come back to it a few days later and group the values into similar areas. For example, "loyalty", "reliability", and "dependability" may go together.
3. Maybe you have 7-10 value groups—look at each and pick one word per group to encapsulate your core personal values.

4

A STATE OF BEING

DO YOU WANT TO "BE SOMEONE" OR "DO
SOMETHING"?

D o you want to be famous, be well known for something, be someone people look up to and want to be like? Like a Kardashian, being famous for being famous? Or do you want to do something of significance for the right reasons, even though you may never be rewarded for it?

Ego drives the need to "be someone", the need for narcissistic recognition to fit in.

The desire to make a difference and help people drives the need to do something of significance for the right reasons. And ironically, the former often results from the latter, anyway. By doing the right things for the right reasons, you end up "being someone".

By trying to fit in, to "be someone" we often modify our behaviour to be the someone we think people want us to be. We imagine what people are thinking and expecting of us and we project this imagined thinking into our own thoughts so we can fit in. It's driven by ego. Imagine acting every day, putting on a face that isn't you so you feel accepted by people you don't even necessarily like. Yet this happens all around us all the time.

The problem with "being someone" is that the outcome of

becoming famous is completely out of our control. We have no control over whether other people will form the opinion that we are "someone". We have no control over their thoughts, beliefs, actions, or feelings.

It's the same with our goals. Focusing on goals that are based on other people's opinions or imagined expectations of us will lead us to reduce our personalities down to what we think (imagine) is socially acceptable. Other people's opinions of you will drive your personality.

There's no freedom, no control, and no integrity in living this way. We become slaves to imagination. That isn't for me, and it surely isn't for you.

We can apply this to your business, too. I've mentioned difficult clients before. If you modify your marketing messages to appeal to as many potential clients as possible, so you fit in and don't upset anyone, you'll simply attract clients that aren't right for you.

Are You Constantly Frustrated?

You are much better off focusing on doing something than being someone. Focus on your actions (do something), rather than results (be someone). Why? Because you have full control over your actions, you decide what you do. You do not control the result of your actions. You do not decide whether someone buys your widget or service. You do not decide whether the long-range shot goes into the back of the net. You do not decide whether your partner likes the dinner you've just made. You do not decide whether the arrow hits the bullseye.

There are myriad external and uncontrollable factors that determine the result, so why focus on them? Get your process right and use results to measure the effectiveness of your process.

This can be a tough pill for business owners to swallow as

it cuts to the core of what we think our role as a business owner is.

Results. Goals. Targets: we're obsessed with them. We set ourselves goals, targets, and results to achieve: turnover (a vanity metric, by the way) must be up by X percent. Profit (the sanity metric) must be up by Y percent. Expenses must go down by Z percent. And so on.

We set ourselves up to fail because we have no control over the target we've set.

Look at the quadrant diagram below as we fill it in together.

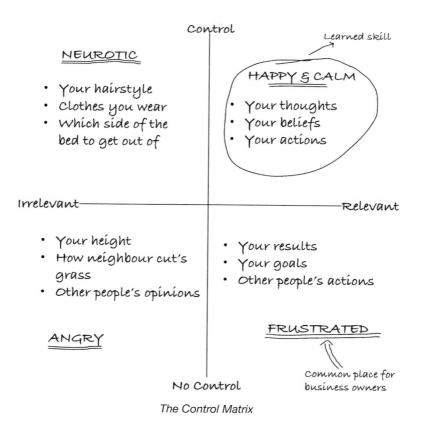

The Control Matrix

At the top, there are things we control and at the bottom are the things we don't control. On the left is stuff that's irrelevant; on the right is stuff that's relevant.

ANGRY! Let's start in the bottom left with stuff we have no control over and which is irrelevant. People living in this quadrant sweat about unimportant stuff they can't control, like their height, how the neighbour cuts the grass, and other people's opinions. They spend their time talking about what so-and-so did or said. So what? Why do they care? It's irrelevant and they have no control over it. People in this sector tend to be angry all the time.

This type of person often exercises coercive control in relationships. They're angry at those around them for "making" them feel a certain way. They're unable to cope with people doing things differently from them, or holding contrary opinions. So, they control. They coerce. They get angry. And sometimes they get abusive.

Some might argue our own actions and our own behaviour affect *their* opinions and hurt *their* feelings. To that I say: most of us have freedom of thought; it's not *1984*. No-one is controlling our thoughts, at least not in our liberal democracy. No-one is making us form a particular opinion. We choose the opinions we hold. Our actions do not result in other people's opinions. Other people decide those opinions for themselves. That's not to say it's a good idea to go around behaving like an arsehole. Just that we each have full control over how we react to other people's behaviour.

People in this bottom-left quadrant often express anger at the way other people do things, insistent that everyone must do and see things their way. Outside of the law, no-one has the right to decide what I do or how I choose to do it. The bottom-left people tend to have a victim mentality: any misfortune is always someone else's fault. They can be depressive, and they are most certainly negative. They focus on the negative stuff in their lives, then blame other people for it. Blame, shame, judgement, and criticism are key character traits.

FRUSTRATED. In the bottom-right quadrant are things we can't control that remain relevant, like results and goals. They are important to us, no doubt about that. Making enough profit to feed the family and invest in your future is relevant, but it is out of our control because we can't force people to buy from us. We don't have control of results, but we do have control of the actions that bring about our results—so focus on your actions and not the results you want to see. As they say in Dubai, "Build it and they will come."

Other people's actions fit into the bottom-right quadrant too. If a competitor is slashing prices and aggressively marketing to your client base, that's relevant—but you have no control over it.

People living in this quadrant are frustrated. They get anxious and panicked about things they can't control, which is a waste of energy. They believe clients hold all the cards. They are permanently frustrated with the weather, the state of the economy, their client's behaviour, and other people's actions. They moan about stuff they can't control and because they focus on goals and results, they remain frustrated because they never achieve their goals. Why? Because they keep taking the same actions yet expect a different result. Pointless.

NEUROTIC. Moving to the top-left, here are things you *can* control, like your hairstyle (unless, like me, you have little hair left), the clothes you wear, which side of the bed you get out of. They're not important in the grand scheme of things, but we do control them.

People living in this quadrant often have neurotic characteristics. They worry about irrelevant things and focus on stuff that adds no material value. They spend oodles of time perfecting the margins on their headed paper. They drag themselves into pointless detail that does nothing to grow their business. They worry about the position of a picture on the wall.

HAPPY & CALM. Then, in the top right, are the people who focus their energy on things they can control and which are relevant to them. They focus on their thoughts, their beliefs, and their actions—because in the end, that's all we can control, all we can influence, and all that is important. This is the only place to put your energy as a business owner.

Putting energy into moaning about the weather, what someone else thinks, or the colour of your shoelaces is a pointless waste of time.

Take Charge of Your Destiny

Now, I don't want to sound trite here because I know this isn't easy. None of us has a magic switch to transform ourselves into one of the top 1% of people in the top-right quadrant. It is a learned skill, and it takes focus, determination, confidence, courage, and integrity to achieve. It's rare to meet someone who focuses 100% of their energy on relevant controllable stuff 100% of the time. We all have lapses. I know I do, every single day.

For example, I get frustrated when a potential client who has booked a meeting with me, doesn't turn up or cancels five minutes beforehand. It's a complete waste of my time and shows lack of respect for other people's time. It's selfish. I used to get properly annoyed and then seek to re-arrange the meeting. Now, I channel that frustration into politely letting them go as a potential client. I do not want or need unreliable clients; they cause more work than they're worth. They've broken my rules before we even begin; rules that keep control of my business, and allow me to run it my way—and which are beneficial for my clients, too.

When I started out in financial advice, I set up under the auspices of one of the UK's largest financial services firms. It was the right thing to do at the time because they provided support mechanisms to help me grow my business. I had access to pre-approved marketing literature, IT systems, training, and the like. This was great at first because it allowed me to focus on helping my clients and improving the advice I gave.

But I quickly became frustrated with the bureaucracy and processes involved in being part of a larger organisation. Professional managers were making decisions that affected my ability to grow my business. I plunged into a negative spiral of frustration which was unhealthy and unhelpful.

The results I wanted didn't materialise because I couldn't take the actions I needed to take to grow my business. As a highly regulated business, control is integral and important and their process worked for them—but I didn't have control over many aspects of *my* business, like how I marketed to clients. I focused my energy in the bottom-right corner of frustration.

My mentor, straight-talking and direct, was pretty clear about the solution: focus on my thoughts, beliefs, and actions and accept the restrictions on the way I could do things—or leave.

I left.

And it was the best thing I ever did. Why? Because I regained control of my business. I can focus on my thoughts, beliefs, and actions. I can establish my own rules and implement them. I can speak to my clients in the way I want to.

I can stop feeling frustrated by other people's actions—and I have the control I need to take the actions I want to produce the results I desire.

Most business owners spend too much time focused on the relevant but uncontrollable. This is perfectly normal so don't beat yourself up about it. We're hard-wired to focus on results and achieve goals, and when we don't get what we want, it's natural to feel frustrated. But the reality is, we don't control the outcome of our actions, only the actions themselves.

Do you still want to "be someone", knowing that you have absolutely no control over whether that outcome will occur? Or do you want to do something, the right thing, even though that may not come with fame and recognition?

How to Start Doing Something

We can't move for mission and vision statements, goals and objectives these days. It's all-pervading, including at home. The whole coaching industry is built on defining goals and helping us reach them. Lifestyle gurus encourage personal mission and vision statements, mood boards, and action plans. Give me a break—it's overwhelming.

And often, it doesn't work, because these plans have nothing concrete behind them to back them up.

Ever written a business plan for the bank or similar? I'll bet a key element was financial targets. At no point will they ask you about your thoughts and beliefs, or your rules and values. They're only ever interested in the outcome, the result, the goal, the target—and the action you're going to take to get there. They're interested in your marketing plan.

But if your thoughts and beliefs, rules and values, do not align with what's written down, well, you can make the loveliest marketing plan in the world, but it'll just be words on a page.

You might have guessed that I have a bit of an issue with business plans and this relentless focus on results. How can you possibly guess what your results are going to be? I understand there are commercial reasons for the bank to want to know how much you're going to turnover or earn, because that's how they make their money; but if your mindset isn't right, the results will never come.

Until you have clarity in your mind, until you have

thoughts, beliefs, and actions that are aligned and tweaked through the measure of results, until you have rules and values that align, you're just writing dreamt-up numbers on a page.

When it comes to setting goals, most people advocate breaking goals down into smaller, shorter-term goals. This sounds useful, and it is to an extent—but the problem is that by doing so we remain focused on the result. There's nothing wrong with this, as long as your thoughts and beliefs, rules and values align with actions that will get you that result—and as long as you actually take those actions.

But simply defining a set of manageable goals and focusing on them isn't always going to get you there.

Do You Swim or Jump?

I like to think about goals in terms of a preference for rivers or islands. Some people have a Big Hairy-Arse Goal in mind for their life. Others don't. Those who do have a BHAG tend to be river people. They often have a grand vision, for themselves and their business, or maybe for the wider world. Those who don't are often island people, and being comfortable is enough for them.

What type of person are you?

Depending on the type of person you are, you'll either follow the river or hop from island to island. More likely, you'll be a mix of both.

Imagine your BHAG is to go into space with Virgin Galactic. You know how much it costs, so it's easy to define. You set yourself goals along the way to help you keep on track. For example:

- Reduce expenditure by 10% per month within six months.
- Get that promotion so you can earn more money.
- Save 20% of the cost of the trip within 12 months.

Each of these goals is an island. By defining stages along the way, you've broken your BHAG into manageable chunks: your personal islands. Because they're smaller and closer, they feel more manageable and thus achievable.

But remember this: to get from one island to the next, you still have to jump in the river and swim. You have to *do* something.

But not everyone thinks like that. There is another valid way: river thinking.

We'll use the same BHAG: to go into space. This time, though, we set our destination—space—and keep our focus firm on swimming towards it. We swim along the river, secure in the knowledge that the river will eventually take us to the sea (our goal). We don't set targets along the way; instead, we focus on the process of swimming and breathing.

We know that if we get the process right, the outcome will look after itself. In other words, if we do the right actions and practice them, we get better and better and closer and closer to our goal. We swim using breast-stroke, for example, and monitor the outcome. Did we swim faster? In the right direction? How tired were we afterwards?

Then we change our stroke—perhaps to front crawl—and monitor the outcome again. Did we do better with front crawl or breast-stroke?

My point is: we focus on the process of getting to the sea. We concentrate on making our journey efficient and profitable, rather than focusing on individual islands along the way.

Instead of breaking our BHAG into smaller chunks and aiming for those, we keep our BHAG at the top of our mind, all the time. Everything we do is aligned with achieving that goal: how we swim, what stroke we use, the course we choose to take. Sometimes we'll take a wrong turn and swim down the wrong branch of the river. But that's okay because all downstream paths will lead to the sea. It might take a little longer, but the process of swimming and breathing will still get us there.

Neither approach—rivers or islands—is right or wrong. They're just different.

The challenge for any coach, advisor, or consultant is to understand which approach is right for you. One size rarely fits all and what is right today may not be right tomorrow.

Finding Your Preference

It's important to find out if you prefer river or island thinking, because if you read a book which tells you to break your goals down into manageable chunks, but you just don't think like that, then the approach will not work for you. And vice versa.

The approach you take may be different for different goals. In some aspects of your life and business, you'll prefer river thinking and in others, you'll prefer island thinking. There is no right and wrong here, just different.

I'm sure there are plenty of (expensive) psychological tests you can take to help determine your natural approach— take one, if that's right for you. However, if you spend some time thinking about the approach you took to a past success, you'll quickly identify your natural preference. Find that preference and understand it as it needs to be congruent with your actions.

If your thoughts, beliefs, and actions align with river thinking and continuous improvement to the Big Hairy Ass Goal, then setting interim goals is going to annoy the hell out of you.

On the other hand, if you do better working towards smaller goals, you may find setting one BHAG overwhelming and intimidating.

Either way, you're going to experience setbacks. The key is to put your energy into moving forward. Take the actions you need to take, and keep evaluating them: are they working for you? Could you improve?

Whatever approach you take, you will need to be resilient if you want to be successful.

Failure is as much a part of business success as success itself.

What's Next?

Remember: what other people think of you is none of your business, and you can't control it, anyway. You can control your thoughts, beliefs and actions, so take personal responsibility for them. Now, as an aside, I understand that those who suffer with conditions like anxiety cannot always control their thoughts and they might need specialist help. But mostly, we get to choose what we think. How cool is that?

Take charge of your thoughts, beliefs, and actions. Focus on the process and measure it with results.

Create your own quadrant and figure out what's important to you and what isn't, what you can control, and what you can't. Then be honest about where you're putting your energy.

Now decide what you want to do, and why.

5

DISCOMFORT AND GRIT
"BRACE! BRACE! BRACE!"

We hit the water with a hefty jolt and start sinking immediately. The vibration and noise as the icy cold water rushes up through the cockpit floor is shocking. It's dark; I can't see much—but I can feel the water rushing up my body and I can feel the aircraft tipping over to the left.

I'm in the left-hand seat: I have milliseconds to take my last breath.

It's cold, damn cold, as the water hits my head and torso. It takes my breath away and I resist the urge to gasp, just as we'd been trained. I grip the cockpit door grab handle with every ounce of strength to keep myself oriented. That way lies my exit; I ejected the cockpit door on our way down. I feel like a rag doll, thrown around as the water and the cockpit meet.

I'm underwater now: lots of bubbles and strangely still noisy. Upside down. Dark. And then silence. Strapped into my seat upside down in the dark, icy water as we sank.

My training kicks in.

I am not going to die today.

But I need air: out comes the STAS bottle[1]. Mouthpiece in, purge water, start breathing. Ish.

I'm upside down so there's a little pool of water in the roof of my mouth. It feels odd. But hey, I'll take odd versus not breathing at all.

Five or six seconds have passed since we hit the water.

My lungs are burning through fear. Pure fear. I'm one big ball of pumped-up adrenalin. Feeling for my harness release, I tug the straps undone and haul myself and my survival seat pack (a one-man life raft) out through the cockpit door, using the grab handle to guide me.

Now, which way is up?

Odd question? No. Because when you sink below about two to five metres, the body becomes negatively buoyant.

I remember Tom[2], one of my compatriots. When I was serving in the Gulf, he died when his aircraft ditched at night in the sea. One second they were flying at 100 feet and 150 miles an hour, the next they smashed into the sea at full speed. Literally zero warning. The Board of Enquiry determined that Tom escaped from the cockpit and used all of his STAS. He cut himself out of his harness, which had become jammed, using the survival J-knife we all carried strapped to our right leg. They think he became disoriented and swam downwards instead of up. He'd cut his lifejacket trying to escape so he couldn't use it to guide him to safety.

So, which way is up?

I recalled my training: feel where the bubbles are going when you breathe out. I followed the bubbles and broke the surface with my survival seat pack attached and all bodily parts functioning.

Success.

Training for the Unexpected

"Well done sirs, a good escape. Lieutenant Smith, you released your harness slightly too early. You must wait until all violent motion has ceased so you remain oriented to your exit and don't start floating about."

"Aye-aye, chief."

I'd just completed my annual "Dunker" drills at RNAS Yeovilton, the home of the Royal Navy Fleet Air Arm where my front-line Lynx helicopter squadron was based. It was just a drill, but a crucial one. The training, the constant reinforcement of what to do in an emergency, drummed into us, saves lives. The process saves lives.

I hated every second.

Even though there are safety divers in there with us, even though we have a three-minute air supply on hand, even though the whole thing takes less than 30 seconds, it put the fear of the devil in me every time.

I mean, we can all hold our breath for 30 seconds, right? Trust me: when the adrenaline is coursing and you're terrified, that breath does not last long.

When I was about 15 or 16, those of us interested in joining the military took a school trip to the Dunker. That was my first experience of the underwater fear and it still frightens me today, despite all the training. But I knew I had to overcome that fear, learn to manage it, and make sure if that situation happened to me, I would survive.

I had that chance shortly before I started my actual flying training. After completing my basic officer training at Dartmouth, I had about three months to wait until I started flying training. I was based at Yeovilton, helping with various activities, so I called the Dunker Chief and asked if I could help him out every week. I explained that I found the Dunker a real challenge (I'd just done my first annual drill) and I needed to build my confidence in the environment.

The chief was, of course, delighted to help.

I spent the next three months, once a week, helping out training school kids, trainee Royal Marine Commandos, seasoned aircrew, and the like.

The Commandos were the ones that helped me realise that being afraid wasn't being weak. It was just being afraid.

These were big, strapping blokes, full of banter and bravado, gung-ho and up for anything—and some of them fell completely to pieces in the Dunker.

Sometimes I'd sit in one of the spare seats in the Dunker, with a mask, to watch them. I became so much more comfortable with the discomfort that it became comfortable.

I'd watch the biggest, burliest macho man lose complete control of his senses the moment the water hit. They'd be out of their seats and out of the window before the water had got to their knees, which is a problem because if it were real, the rotor blades would mash them.

Screaming like children at a soft play, some of them! It would have been funny if it wasn't so serious.

But I also watched them help each other stay calm, rationalise the experience, and stay focused. I saw their camaraderie and the trust they have in each other spelled out clearly in that underwater cage.

I saw why the British Armed Forces remain so revered around the world.

And I learned that I had nothing to fear but fear itself. I learned the importance of grit, determination and resilience.

I learned that comfort only comes on the far side of discomfort.

It's always been that way; ever since the day we were born.

Embracing Discomfort

Do you remember your first birthday? No, of course not. Do you remember learning to walk, constantly falling over, toppling backwards, knocking your head, scraping your knees? No, of course not. But you still kept trying. You kept at it.

You had resilience, determination, and grit.

Almost all business owners need resilience, determination, and grit because running a business is not for the faint-hearted. Unlike regular employment where you still get paid when you get it wrong, if we get it wrong in our business, we may lose the client and the income. There's much more on the line when we own a business, so we need a good helping of grit, determination, and resilience.

Yet many business owners have forgotten what it's like to learn to walk. You have to take some knocks before you master it.

How we deal with the knocks is the measure of our future success. You can see a "failure" as evidence of why something will not work, and fall victim to confirmation bias, or you can learn a valuable lesson from it. Failure is only failure when we decide its failure. For the successful business owners, failure is a test that helps us learn.

As with most things in business, this all comes down to attitudes and beliefs, our experiences and our mindset. If you seek comfort, then comfort is what you'll get. It makes me think of a conversation I had with my wife, Beverley.

We both like the colder months. We like the crisp air of winter, cosy log fires, mulled wine, and blankets. Beverley wraps up to the eyeballs when we go out, so not an ounce of freezing air gets through. I prefer to feel the cold air. I embrace the discomfort of it on my ears because I want to experience it. I don't want to be so wrapped up and comfortable that I lose the ability to feel. Discomfort is an integral part of the winter experience for me.

For the same reasons, I like to seek new experiences that prod me out of my comfort zone and gently nudge me to test my boundaries.

Much of this passion stems from my military training, of that I have no doubt. In training, they always pushed us and eventually we learned to push ourselves.

For a while I ran a four-week leadership course for young Naval Officers. They struggled with their confidence, fitness, or attitude, or sometimes all three. The purpose of the course was to turn them around and get them back into mainstream training, and give them a chance to succeed.

For 80 percent of them, the issue was always confidence. Mainstream training can only do so much; some people need a little more attention to help push them past their limiting beliefs.

When they arrived on that course, their confidence was at the lowest possible ebb. They'd just failed the primary leadership test on Dartmoor and been back-coursed. It was too humiliating for some, and they quit there and then. I didn't persuade them to stay. I shook their hands, wished them well, and pointed them to the Training Office for discharge from the Navy. They needed resilience and passion for my course and the reward was fun (some of the time!).

Those who stayed saw a lot of me. I did everything with them. Every exercise, every run, every challenge, every sleepless night. I watched them transform from timid kids into capable young leaders, which was exhilarating to see. It was a gruelling schedule:

- Week one: pack your bags, we're going on a 5-day expedition. Here's the kit list, you've got one hour, bring your passport. Lesson: learn to deal with uncertainty—discomfort.
- Week two: "You've worked hard tonight, well done. You can have a lie-in in the morning: 6.05 am for a run." We usually start at 6 am. Laughs and groans. Lesson: you still have to get up and do the job —resilience.
- Week three: "You four, I'd like you to climb that telegraph pole, all stand on the top, hold hands, and lean out together." The pole had a 30cm square plate on top. Lesson: confidence, trust, and teamwork.
- Week four: running towards the sea (in December).

"Keep going, don't stop until you're up to your thighs, then get under the water." Lesson: I needed to wash my kit. Just joking. Lesson: if you can put up with freezing cold December sea water, you can do anything.

Feeling the Cold

I remember my first experience of running into the cold sea. I was just 16 and on a three-week outward bound course with the Army in Wales. I remember the feeling well.

I felt *alive*.

My head and body tingled from the cold saltwater and exercise. I felt like I could do anything. Boy, did that do a lot for my teenage confidence. I was a different person when I came home.

Even now, I'll sometimes have a cold shower to sharpen my senses when there's something I need to do that I don't want to do, or that I find uncomfortable. Like networking. I hate networking. The prospect of walking into a room to network with people I've never met before fills me with complete and utter dread. Ridiculous really, as I'm a perfectly sociable person. It's the thought of it that bothers me; the reality has always been enjoyable. Makes absolutely no sense does it?

The point is this. You need to experience discomfort; you need to push yourself in ways that are uncomfortable. By doing so, you will truly learn about grit, resilience, and determination, and learn to apply that to your business and personal life.

My stories are pretty extreme; most people don't experience military training. But you don't need to go to extremes to push yourself and experience discomfort. A cold shower in the morning can get the job done.

The rest of this chapter contains some stories that shaped

who I am, that gave me the resilience and determination to overcome challenges and be the person I am today.

Survival

One of the first courses we do before we start flying training is survival training. It's for special forces and aircrew only, as we're more likely to find ourselves in an unpleasant situation, fending for ourselves, with information in our heads—and we're a valuable resource given the vast cost of training (many multi-millions of pounds). It's a four-week course, extremely arduous and, at times, most unpleasant.

It begins with daily exercise delivered by military survival experts, mostly ex-SAS or Royal Marines who've completed and passed SAS selection. Holy crap. I've never been so knackered in my life. Those boys are fit, damn fit. Then you get the classroom training about mushrooms, eating off the land and survival priorities. Even now, the mantra stays in my head: protection, location, water, and food.

The vast majority of rescues around the world happen within the first 24 hours, be that military or civilian. You can survive 24 hours without water, much longer without food, so the survival priority is protection from the elements that can kill or debilitate you (sun, cold) followed by location for rescue.

Location training helps people find you. They taught us how to build smoke fires and have them ready to go and other techniques for signalling location, some covertly. They taught us escape and evasion techniques, hiding, how to move at night and lay up in the day. We learned how to get away from dogs and helicopters. And then we put the training into practice on an eight-day assessed exercise in the New Forest.

It starts with a naked examination to make sure we're not smuggling contraband, like cash, onto the exercise. In our small group of four, we split into pairs, and then we're on our own—just as the weather was turning cold, in a pair of overalls and jumper, with a knife and tobacco tin full of survival essentials: flint and steel, snare, condom (water carrier), tampon (cotton wool for fire lighting), and curry powder (to make the food you find palatable). I still have my tin, bashed into a slight oval shape to maximise space for contents, and with most of the contents still within. Not sure I'll be needing it anymore! Hopefully not at any rate.

We foraged and caught our own food. You have to understand we had next to no food for eight days; we'd eat anything we found by day two. We found a beef steak mushroom, and they gave us a live chicken to prepare. If you're squeamish, move on to the next paragraph. I have seen the saying in action: running around like a headless chicken.

From mid-week, they up the ante. No more cooking, no more fires, we're covert now. There's some movement by night. Night and day observation posts, each taking watches. We lay up in the day. I remember laying up inside a huge gorse and bramble bush, four of us snuggled up, one snoring (which required frequent kicks). It was fine until we realised we were at a popular walking and picnicking spot; people were picking blackberries not two feet away from us with no idea we were there. It had benefits though, because we found a half-eaten sandwich to share. Delicious.

We ate raw sweetcorn off the cob from the field; we picked raw onions and ate them like apples; we foraged through bins for anything we could find. An out-of-date jar with two pickled eggs in it: thank you very much. I hate vinegar and I hate eggs, but I still ate my half. You have no idea what it's like to move 10-15 miles at night, without a torch, come rain, wind or cold, covertly and on an empty stomach. As an exercise in mental determination, it beats anything I've ever done by a long way.

Then we're into pairs for a couple of days. It gets harder, as if it wasn't hard enough already! There's more ground to cover at night. Fewer shelter opportunities. Trying to sleep at 4 am in a shallow ditch in a wood in early October with nothing but your overalls and a jumper is not fun. Ben and I, we cuddled like a loving couple for that few hours of snatched existence. It's the first, last, and only time I've spooned with a man. It was so worth it because we were absolutely bloody freezing. I have no idea how we got through to mid-morning.

And then I'm alone. Now I'm being chased. It might only be an exercise, but it feels mighty real. The hairs on the back of my neck are standing up and I have goosebumps as I write this. There's genuine fear as I suddenly hear the dogs barking and a helicopter approaching.

It's giving me the shivers just remembering it.

Everyone eventually gets caught. By this time, we're so weak and exhausted that we just can't run very fast. The final stage is classified—or the details are, at least. I can tell you what's in the public domain: resistance to interrogation. Google it yourself. You might have seen some RTI stuff on the Special Forces programmes on the BBC.

Trust me, that's barely scratching the surface of what we went through.

Looking back, I learnt a vast amount about myself during those eight days in the field. It's only when you're truly pushed to your limits you begin to understand your own mind, your own strengths and weaknesses, and your own mental and physical limits.

Sink and You'll Swim

Two days later, bathed and showered, rested and well fed, it's onto the next course. Damage control, firefighting, and respirator training (operating in a chemical warfare environment). That was fun, respirator training. Not.

Into the gas chamber lads! Set off the tear gas. Get your gas mask on and practice your drills. Tear gas is properly minging when it gets into your throat and eyes.

Damage control was much more fun. Genuinely. I found it interesting, and I enjoyed it, although it was frightening at times. We entered a burning metal inferno in full firefighting kit and oxygen to put out the fire, simulating a fire emergency at sea, or the aftermath of a missile attack.

Big respect to firefighters. I know they have better kit now, but that was damn hot. They show you what happens with back draft, how to boundary cool to stop fire spreading, how to protect your team and the ship as you enter a fire-filled compartment to put the blaze out. You can't just leave fire to burn on a ship. It's something we practised most days at sea too; not with actual fire, but they drilled the procedures into us. Fire is one of the biggest dangers at sea.

Then came the DRIU[3]. The dreaded DRIU. The Damage Repair Instructional Unit. Imagine we're at sea and we hit a rock. We've got water pissing in through a hole in the side of your ship. We can't just leave it—and it'll take more than a finger to plug it. So, we train for it in a mock-up ship. On hydraulic rams. It's a great big house-sized simulator. In we go, with a bag of wooden wedges, a hammer and a head torch.

"Brace! Brace! Brace!"

It's a simulated missile attack. And then the water starts pissing in through the holes in the compartment and the hydraulic rams simulate the ship rolling and turning. The water isn't a dribble, either. It's coming at us fast through multiple holes, some small (4-6 inches), some large (12 inches). As a team, we try to plug the holes. Including the ones in the floor.

That's quite a challenge when the water rises to your chest. So, we take it in turns to hold each other down underwater to do the wedging and hammering. It's cold water, too; they don't waste money heating it! Deep breath, wedge in one hand, hammer in the other—and my mate holds me under for the count of 30. Eventually we lose the battle of course and we have to decide when to evacuate the compartment before the water breaches the next deck.

Chilly, but good fun.

Staying Positive

It would be easy to face the challenges I shared above with fear and trepidation in your heart and mind. I definitely had some of those feelings, and more—but I never once doubted my ability to do it.

Yes, I had to push myself. Yes, I had to overcome fear and anxiety. Yes, I was scared at times.

But right from day one, the military instils a positive sense of self-worth and a can-do attitude. The teamwork and camaraderie are second-to-none, and I don't believe you can experience anything like it anywhere else.

Some people liken military camaraderie to a close-knit sports team. I get that, but there is a difference: sport generally isn't life and death.

Quite literally, I put my life in the hands of other people when I joined the military. It isn't a choice; it's a necessity. There are very few walks of life that push you to the limits I've experienced, that really challenge our minds, our bodies, and our spirits, that stretch the boundaries of what we believe to be possible.

I've talked already about the importance of a positive mindset. As you say it, so it shall become. If you truly believe you can do it, you will. That is not the same as entitlement. It is not the same as growing up being told you can do anything. You can achieve anything you want, but you have to work at it. It will not land at your feet because you think you're entitled to it.

Simon Sinek talks about entitlement in one of his videos, and it's well worth a watch. There's some generalisation in the interview, but it's an interesting view on how some people think, young or old.

"Entitled" is a label often given by the older generation to younger people. It's unhelpful, because labels can be a self-fulfilling prophecy. If we repeatedly tell youngsters that they are entitled, they'll believe us and act accordingly.

A positive mindset is essential for our own success, as business owners and leaders. But we must be careful about the labels we assign to ourselves and to our employees, and the way we talk to ourselves and to others. Those labels, and the words we speak and the attitudes we embody will self-fulfil.

We have to model what we want to see. If you want positive employees with a rounded outlook who work hard in your business to make a difference to people's lives, then you need to live, work and breathe those values yourself.

Your business and how your employees feel about their work is entirely down to you. My business and its success is entirely down to me. Yes, there are outside influences we can't control, but how we respond to them and approach challenges is down to us.

You must take personal responsibility for your leadership, for the decisions you make and how that plays out for your employee and client relationships. I don't always get it right because I'm a human being—and despite thinking we make logical decisions; we don't. We act on impulse and with emotion, even the stalwart rugged individuals, whether they'll admit it or not.

Given that very human trait, all we can do is stay positive about our prospects, believe in ourselves, and act accordingly. Your results will reflect how successful you are at doing so.

What's Next?

So, what are you going to do today to stretch yourself? I don't mean yoga or Pilates! How are you going to experience discomfort? What action will you take to make sure your mindset is positive? Here are a couple of ideas:

1. You don't have to go to the extremes I did to push yourself into discomfort every day. Start small: take a cold shower in the morning. See what difference it makes. If nothing else, everything that follows will be much more comfortable...

2. Remember: failure is just a test with results you didn't like. Use it as a learning experience and it'll never be a waste of time and effort.

3. We're not entitled to success: it comes from grit, determination, and hard work. Which means you are in control. How great is that?

6

RUGGED INDIVIDUALS

WE'RE NOT MEANT TO DO THIS ALONE

Do you take the red pill or the blue pill?

This is a scene from the movie *The Matrix* which I found both entertaining and thought-provoking. The movie is about a world run by machines who harvest human beings as batteries. The matrix is the machine-generated virtual world in which the harvested humans "live" to maintain their effectiveness as batteries for the machines.

The film is as much about control and feeling in control as it is about living in a virtual world. Most of the humans living in the virtual world, the matrix, are happily oblivious to their reality as a battery. But some of them like to challenge the status quo, explore why, ask questions, and seek understanding.

Their understanding doesn't come from taking the red pill. That just opens their eyes. Understanding only comes from within.

It took a good five years for me to realise there is no pill for getting your head straight and your mental health sorted; not that I ever tried any mind-numbing drugs other than alcohol. Perhaps that's why so many people resort to drugs and substance abuse to numb their internal pain. There are no simple answers to all this.

I'm an ex-military type, so being the stalwart, rugged individual—unfazed, unmoved, and unemotional—was all I knew. As Beverley, my wife, says, "Stable, dependable, reliable... and boring." Still, stiff upper lip and all that; cricket and cucumber sandwiches, wear the right thing, do the right thing, meet other people's expectations, even if those expectations are of my own imagining, projections of what I thought they wanted from me.

Except I wasn't happy inside. I sort of knew that, whilst refusing to accept it. I didn't know what to do about it, so I pressed on with being rugged. They say no man is an island, but I was trying to be. I now realise the expectations I was desperately trying to live up to were entirely of my own making. Nobody was actually looking at me and judging me if I didn't do something, if I didn't achieve "greatness", or if I took a rest.

The only person judging me, was me.

I was closed to who I really am. I was living the socially expected norm of life, climbing the corporate ladder, earning more, buying more, living faster and, ultimately, probably dying younger. Despite a continuing interest in learning new things, reading books, exploring new ideas, and having adventures, I remained closed to me. Closed to who I was, to my personality, trapped in social expectations. I was caught up in the social media echo chamber, believing that success and happiness are worn like badges of honour on your sleeve, depicted in the car you drive or the house you live in, the holidays you take.

I look back now and think, "Dickhead." Or, as my wife puts it, "Mid-life crisis." Whatever label you want to put on it, I was well and truly in it.

Blame, Shame, Judgement, and Criticism

Knowing something isn't right is one thing, doing something about it is quite another.

Of course, the rugged individual in me just thought, "It's not me, it's them." Whoever "them" was. Blame.

And then came shame. Judgement. Criticism. And ego.

And then I discovered Brené Brown. Well, I say *I* discovered her. My wife did. And forced me to listen to her. Yes, forced. I resisted heavily, convinced there was nothing wrong with me, it was everyone else.

In our family, whoever is driving chooses the tunes; it's an unwritten rule. Although I wryly note that only seems to apply when I'm driving on my own... A few years ago, Beverley was driving, so she chose the tunes. Except she chose an Audible book by Brené Brown: *The Power of Vulnerability*. I was not enamoured at the prospect of some hippy left-wing cuddly BS telling me to go hug a tree and I'll feel better.

I was "forced" to listen for maybe an hour, I guess.

Dr Brené Brown is an American psychologist who researches shame. What on earth does that mean? Yep, that's what I thought too. What the hell is shame? Do you mean feeling ashamed and this is just the American translation? I really didn't get it at all.

I was intrigued and interested, though, as I found the content compelling if completely unintelligible. So, I resolved to listen to the book on my commute. I had a 90-minute commute every day back then, so I finished the book in a week.

By Friday, I still hadn't got a clue what she was talking about, but I remained interested. So, I listened to the whole thing again the next week. It was starting to make sense. I began to understand that when we feel judged or criticised (note use of the word "feel"), we fall into shame. And shame is a bad place to be. Shame is our inner devil.

Shame is that shitty part inside us that fights back, irrationally. It's our fight-or-flight mode. The bit that "makes" us say and do stupid things, which we then feel ashamed of. That's shame.

You're now being the dickhead, all because you're feeling shame.

We all have that part inside us, it's just that most people are completely unaware of it and what it does. Without awareness, though, there can be no cure.

The good news is, we can change. We can let go of the box we feel society is constraining us in. We can embrace our personality with gay abandon, and we can say fuck and shit a million times if we want to.[1]

You can be yourself and let go of any concern you have about other people's opinions. I tell you; it is most refreshing when you finally reach that nirvana.

Or, you can stay where you are.

We all know the sort of people who talk only of themselves and how great they are. Donald Trump is the most obvious and famous example. They've usually got a massive chip on their shoulder and they feel inadequate and unworthy. They feel the need to constantly prove themselves to everyone around them; they show off; they are full of bluster and bravado about their achievements. They often suffer from imposter syndrome, although they're unlikely to recognise it because of the size of their inflated ego.

You may have elements of this inside you, and that's perfectly okay. I did. I was in trouble. There's no need to judge yourself, though. If you recognise any of these traits, please start by reading some Brené Brown at least twice. Start with *The Power of Vulnerability*, then read *Men, Women and Worthiness*.

We all know people who have some of these traits and who will probably never accept there is anything "wrong" with them, that they could change or improve who they are. They're the sort of people who talk about themselves a lot, gob off about how much money they have, how big their house is, how fast their car is, how important they are (in their own minds!). You know who I mean. Maybe you can think of a few people you know who fit this description.

The more I learn and understand about shame, the more shame behaviour I see around me. In the pub, at the school gates, in the news, in the media. Think about our current political landscape: it's all about knocking your rival, shaming them. It's so terribly unhealthy.

An Extreme Case of Shame

I'll tell you a story about a chap I met a few years ago. I was well into my shame journey with Brené and other experts by then. I introduced myself and what followed was a fascinating shame case study.

There's a tiny part of me as I write this that wants to describe him as a "dickhead", but I know that's not fair. What I feel most of all is sadness. Sadness because he clearly isn't happy inside and doesn't know what to do about it. I also know he isn't ready (or perhaps willing) to see he has a problem and do anything about it. It is a great shame, excuse the pun, because I'm sure that beneath the ridiculous bravado is a perfectly pleasant person desperate to be let loose.

For 30 minutes, I listened to an egotistical diatribe about himself. How he'd had no father figure in his life until he started being mentored by the owner of a firm he worked for. How he had issues at school and was excluded (read bully). He had a troubled childhood.

He told me how this mentor had taken him under his wing and shown him how to make money. And then there were his rules (which are a good thing actually, and which I'll come back to in the next chapter). It wasn't so much the rules as the arrogant way in which he delivered them and told his stories: "I've got these rules, yeah, and I never break them, yeah?" His statements were always looking for approval with an offhand "yeah?" Not that he'd recognise it as that.

He had rules like, if you arrive in a Range Rover it gets no credit with him. I have no idea what that means and what on earth driving a Range Rover has to do with his business. Absolutely nothing.

His wife bought a Range Rover a few months later which made me chuckle.

I remember asking how he was finding the Range Rover (the Velar), thinking I wouldn't let that first experience colour my judgement. He was just trying to find his position. I was sure he'd be fine, given time. His response was classic ego and shame: "Well, it's a girl's car init. I ain't driving that." Crikey. I nodded sagely and moved on to what I thought would be safer ground.

"How's the house hunting going?" I asked. Well, he couldn't find anything he liked. In fact, he told me about one house in a local village he'd been to see. I knew the one, very nice million-plus pad. "Well, I told the agent, didn't I, I'm not livin' in a million pound 'ouse surrounded by four hundred grand houses, yeah."

Holy macaroni. I kept well away from that point on.

It's been interesting to watch as the years unfold. I see him standing on his own more and more, on his phone. He's not doing anything important, just trying to look important, trying to hide behind his device. Feeling inadequate. Unworthy. I hear that nobody talks to him in the village where he lives. I can't imagine why.

The last time I saw him, he was still pontificating about his own importance. He was describing the importance of soft skills when interviewing candidates. It's a perfectly valid point, finished with a flurry of ego. He did this by telling all and sundry how he has a five-stage interview process for anyone earning over £100k in his business, which culminates in a pint

7

SCHOOL RULES

HOW TO TAKE BACK CONTROL OF YOUR BUSINESS AND YOUR LIFE

When my first child was born in 2009, we insisted we would not be slaves to the television. "We will not be the sort of parents who stick their kids in front of the telly all day."

Well, that didn't last long.

We soon broke that rule. As soon as the television entertained him, our son was in front of it because we were broken. Properly broken. And that was entirely our own fault. Why? Because we didn't set rules. When we did set rules, we didn't enforce them, and we didn't have any set routine. We were, like most new parents, run ragged, exhausted, sleep deprived, and desperate for a break.

We have a set routine now and we restrict the kids' screen time, but it is damned hard to enforce when you want some peace and quiet! Setting the rules and establishing clear boundaries was the most important step we took in taking back control of our lives. The same applies to your business.

We first experience rules as children when our parents teach us to wash our hands before tea, do our homework before play, not to hit our siblings etc... (Although I'm not sure many of us with siblings ever heeded that last rule!) The rules of society are further reinforced in school and higher education. We then enter the workplace where there are rules about when we start, the hours we work, what we wear, etc... As we approach retirement, we are subject to government rules on our pensions. Even when we're dead, there are rules about what happens to our money and our bodies. The simple fact is, we're surrounded by rules.

These rules are there for a reason. They provide structure, certainty, and a common framework for society to operate within. We know what the rules are and most of us stick to them. Most people need that structure to help them feel safe in an otherwise uncertain and chaotic world.

If we look at most parenting books, they talk about routine, consistency, and structure to help a child feel secure in their environment. We also know that setting clear boundaries for children is a good thing.

So, if boundaries are so good, why don't we have them in our businesses? And if we *do* have them, why do we then ignore them?

No Exceptions

Most business owners start out with good intentions. We plan to stick to the rules we set, but then we make just one exception... and before we know it, the exception becomes the rule.

Remember the first time you gave a discount? I bet you do it all the time now and I bet you started out by saying you wouldn't ever give a discount. Oops. Another rule broken. The reality is, most business owners are floundering with no clear idea of what they're doing, why they're doing it, or where they're going—so they don't have clear rules. And that's okay. You're not alone. But you do have to recognise that's what's happening before you can fix it.

Plus, it's hard to say no to people.

I was the same. I'm not immune to this. I still find it hard to say no when clients ask for my same service excellence and quality for a cheaper price, but it gets easier with time. I feel guilty because I want to help, and I want people to feel pleased. Changing these habits, changing how we think, feel, and act is not easy. It takes considerable effort, focus, and attention and you'll still make mistakes along the way.

That's why it's so important to work with someone who'll hold you accountable, who will hold you to your rules when you waver. Because we can't do these things on our own. I remember being clear to myself about discounts: I would never offer them. And I broke the rule with my very first client. It doesn't happen now, though. I might still feel guilty, but my rules mostly prevent clients who expect discounts ever getting near me.

I do this by being clear and up-front, setting clear expectations and defining our relationship from the outset. All prospective clients have a 30-minute discovery call with me. The purpose is to understand a little more about the problem they're facing, why they're coming to me and why now, and for them to understand how I work, and what they can expect from me.

If the prospective client expects a discount at the outset, not only do I say no, I say no to working with them at all. There are excellent reasons for this: my experience shows that the client who seeks something for nothing before we even start is a challenge to work with in the future. You end up with a testy client relationship. A client who doesn't respect the value you bring, doesn't respect your rules (it is *your* business, not theirs), and who expects to pay less than everyone else is not a good client. It is unfair on the other clients to allow one person to pay less, and it does not happen in my business.

It goes deeper than that, though. Consider the client who has seen all my marketing and is aware of my rules and how I operate before the discovery call. Yet they still ask for a discount. I could blame them for being poor clients, say no and walk away—or I can take personal responsibility. The fact is, if someone is asking for a discount then I've failed to demonstrate value. So, whilst I will of course still say no to the discount and to working with them at all, there is no blame, shame, judgement, or criticism. There is only personal responsibility. I recognise that I must use the opportunity to understand how and why I didn't show value, and correct it.

This is a great example of how thoughts, beliefs, and actions lead to results. Here, the result is a failure to demonstrate value. I need to go back to my thoughts, beliefs, and actions to understand where the process needs to change so I get a different result. This leads to incremental improvement and more of the right clients starting their journey to personal sovereignty and affluent prosperity.

Strong rules that suit you will support your business and define your boundaries so you can measure your success. If your rules aren't clear, your only real measure of success becomes profit, and that is out of your control.

Setting and enforcing rules gives you control of your business, control of the actions you take, and the ability to measure the success of your process. It stops you focusing on results that you cannot control (profit) because you don't have a process you do control (thoughts, beliefs, and actions).

It's Your Business—You Set the Rules

Setting boundaries so other people's actions don't violate you and your business is important. Boundaries set the tone for your life and lifestyle. They set the tone for who is in charge.

Think about what that means for a minute. How much do you value your ability to make decisions in your business? How much do you respect your own time and energy? Setting boundaries allows you to protect your time, energy, and decision-making ability. This ties right back to mindset, control, freedom, thoughts, beliefs, and actions. If we allow someone to do something we don't like, they'll continue to do it.

If you allow a client to pay you late, they'll continue to do so because you've allowed it to happen and accepted it as a reasonable way to behave. Now, we can choose to feel frustrated or angry. We can blame, shame, judge, and criticise. Or we can take personal responsibility.

This isn't about victim-blaming; you are not responsible for a client's poor behaviour towards you. But you do have the power to pull them up on it and refuse to accept such behaviour in the future.

People will treat you how you allow them to. If you let poor behaviour go once, it will probably happen again. That's on you. So, let them go (fire them) or ask them to pay up-front before you do any further work.

It's your business. You set the rules.

A good friend of mine told me a story about when he first learned to set rules in his business. One of his clients was a decent chap, and he made good money from working with him... when he paid. It might be six, nine, or even twelve months late. He'd be constantly chasing for payment and because he'd permitted his client to treat him like that, the client carried on doing exactly the same thing: paying late. Eventually, my friend wrote to his client explaining that he had never paid a single bill on time and that could not continue. Then he fired the client using Lord Sugar's words, and told him not to bother paying the outstanding bill. Cathartic.

It's not just about getting paid on time. It's about reducing the stress and workload in your business. It's about finding freedom. The client who pays you late is draining your mental energy because you have to remember to chase them (which is an unpleasant task), compose the email, manage your cash flow, book the invoice (unpaid) in the accounts, and potentially pay corporation tax on it before you receive the money.

You might have a client who pays promptly, but who sends you the documentation you need at the deadline, or late. That client is creating additional work for you and your team, and draining you of energy and profit. To find your freedom, set and maintain rules that ensure your freedom. That can only come from you.

Imagine if you didn't have any rules and imagine your business was a child's nursery. How long do you think you'd survive without rules? The kids would run riot, the parents would come and go whenever they like, no-one would pay you on time, and your administration burden would become unbearable.

It's no different in any business. Your rules are your boundaries. They exist because you decide you want to work in a particular way. They exist because you seek freedom to run your business your way. They exist to give you personal sovereignty and affluent prosperity.

The fact that client X wants you to work differently is none of your business. If they don't like it, they can find someone else. And there'll always be another great client around the corner for you, if you market to them well.

You decide.

Freedom and Control

We all started our lives with rules, from our parents and from school, and those rules continue to influence us every day. We're used to following rules, even if we don't always like it. Many business owners leave regular jobs to start their own businesses, often out of frustration with rules they don't like. Why? Because many business owners like to challenge the status quo, they like to do things differently, they like to be contrary. They seek freedom and control over their own lives.

Yet they completely ignore all control measures by not setting any rules for their business and thus achieve no sovereignty. Worse still, they set rules and then ignore them! Weird, isn't it?

This has more to do with freedom. We want the freedom to operate our businesses our way, so we rebel against the rules-based model we came from. Because we don't like rules, we avoid them in our business, believing a no-rules rule will give us freedom.

And that's perfectly understandable.

But I'm not saying we should have the same rules we rebelled against; I'm saying we should make our own rules. Our rules, created to suit our needs, gives us the sovereignty we're looking for.

Give some thought to the most frustrating aspects of your business and then ask yourself if you want that frustration in your life. Probably not. You probably started your business to feel free and yet you feel more like a servant to your business. Your business is running amok, like an uncontrolled and free-willed teenager, your business is running the show. That is not freedom. That is not control.

Now you've identified the most frustrating aspects of your business, ask what rule you could put in place that would entirely remove those frustrations. It's not easy, and it requires a leap of faith. But it's worth it. Remember, all you're doing is changing the process to seek a different result. That process starts with your thoughts, then your beliefs, and finally the actions you take.

Rule #1: I take control of my time

I used to spend the early days in my business trying to get client work done whilst being constantly interrupted by the telephone. It might be clients, salespeople, suppliers, providers, or other such administrative calls. They were often necessary —but I didn't have to deal with it there and then.

I had no control over my time because I was nurturing an

internal belief that I had to answer the telephone right away. I couldn't let it ring and go to voicemail in case it was "important". The telephone was in charge of the results in my business, but the more interruptions there were, the less effective I was at completing the things I needed to do that day. I'd end up working late with more stress, less time, and less freedom.

All I had to do was stop answering the telephone, but I was held back by a thought that I needed to answer it, a belief that they expected me to answer it, and a process (action) that had me actually answer it. The result was frustration, inefficiency, more stress, less time, and less freedom. This is not what I wanted when I started my business.

And if a client called, I would definitely take the call. Invariably, my client would ask me something I didn't have an answer for off the top of my head. I have lots of clients and I can't remember everything about all of them (which is why I have a system to help me) and the questions are often complex.

This would lead to me dropping whatever I was doing and going down that client's rabbit hole, promising to get back to them tomorrow and doing exactly that. At which point, I wouldn't be able to get hold of them and when I finally did, they'd say thanks, but things have moved on, so I think we're okay now.

Right. Good use of my time.

I'd suffer because I'd still have to get the other client work done and it was clear the question they had asked me hadn't been necessary. The issue had gone away by itself before I'd had time to answer it!

I recognised this was a fundamental frustration for me, so I took personal responsibility for it. I created the situation. I allowed my clients to keep me at their beck and call. I allowed them to ask me anything they wanted, whenever they wanted (including evenings and weekends) and I'd drop everything (including quality time with my wife and children) to answer as quickly as possible, only to find it wasn't that important after all.

The only way to change this frustrating result was to change my thoughts, beliefs, and actions. I had to change my process.

So I stopped answering the telephone.

Sounds simple, huh? But it isn't simple when your whole being revolves around thoughts and beliefs that the telephone needs to be answered as soon as it rings.

Now, you can't just refuse to answer the telephone with no means of follow-up. I also realised many of the questions and queries I received were unnecessary. I needed to put a process in place that would permit the important to get through and allow the unimportant to fall away.

To do this, I called on the support of a mentor and a fantastic group of like-minded people facing similar issues. The benefit of my accountability group was immeasurable, because I wasn't on my own trying to find this answer—and trying to find the strength to implement my rules. This had all been done before using tools. And along came Calendly. (There are other providers, but I use Calendly and Acuity Scheduling.)

Calendly is an online scheduling system that allows clients to see your calendar availability and book a call with you. It links to your Outlook calendar, or Gmail, or whatever you use, to see when you're available. It shows your availability to clients so they can book time with you. You can block hours, days, or weeks out of your diary, and you can tell Calendly not to allow call bookings on Tuesdays and Fridays for example. It's flexible, to meet your own personal and business needs.

I tested it. One client tended to call me whenever a new question came to mind—then often I couldn't find him when I had the answer. I asked my PA to direct the client to book a call with me, rather than putting them through to me. It worked a treat. My client didn't book calls for those brain-farts —and when they did book a call, it was for something important, and I could provide the answer there and then. How? Because the Calendly booking process allows me to ask a simple question of my client: "What can I help you with on our call?"

The booking process clarifies that I spend time preparing for our call, and that it's important to provide me with the context so we can make the best use of our time. This means I know what the problem is in advance, and I can prepare. Because they book the call in my diary in advance, I can plan my day effectively—which means I'm not distracted from other client work.

The result was incredible for me and my business: such a simple solution and a great result for just $12 per month.

The immense frustration I felt with constant interruption, and the consequences for stress, time, and family life, faded away. All because I set a simple rule, "I don't answer the telephone." I put a process in place that works for me, works for my clients, and manages everyone's time effectively.

I can't tell you what your rules should be as they'll be particular to your business and your frustrations, but I can share some of my rules, together with the reasons for them. My experiences may help you identify frustration in your business and help you decide how to overcome them.

Rule #2: I won't support debt to pay my fees

I'm in the business of affluent prosperity. "Affluent prosperity" broadly means earning more than you spend, thus giving you the financial means to invest in your future. Taking on more debt isn't investing in your future. If you can't afford a service, you shouldn't be buying it. It would be professionally repugnant of me to ignore the fact that a client is taking on more debt to try to rescue their situation. More debt is rarely the answer when debt is the problem.

So, I have a rule. "I'll not support debt to pay my fees."

You might think, surely it's none of my business how my clients choose to pay me? You're welcome to think that, but to be honest, your opinion on the matter is none of *my* business because it is my rule and it is my business. I will not be party to a client increasing their debt burden in a desperate attempt to rescue their situation. There is always another way.

Rule #3: No client work on evenings and weekends

I used to work on evenings and weekends, and it wreaked havoc with my family life. I thought working such long hours was necessary. I thought my clients would only be available to see me on weekends and evenings because of their own work. I thought I needed to be absolutely flexible to meet their needs.

My approach caused an enormous amount of extra work, which added to my personal stress. I also recognised it as a thinking error: I thought I had to be flexible, with no evidence to support it. I believed all financial consultants worked evenings and weekends. So, I acted accordingly. It was total nonsense, of course.

I don't do that anymore. I've put systems and processes in place that mean I don't have to work evenings and weekends and my clients get just as good, if not a better service, than they had before. This is because I have more time, more freedom, and more control to spend my time doing the right things and not chasing my tail. If I do work an evening or at the weekend, it's because I want to and not because I have to.

I understand this approach might not suit everyone, and that's okay. There are plenty of financial advisers who are desperate enough or willing to work whatever hours their clients demand to secure a discounted fee. But that's not for me.

The extra fees I may bring in by working longer hours do not make up for lost time. I can always earn more money; whereas time with family and friends is priceless.

I hope my rules gave you a few ideas about rules you can implement in your business, because your business needs rules too and you need to stick to them. Your rules will be different to mine, they will be unique to your needs and wants.

In the Appendices at the end of this book, I've shared my rule book with you. Take a look if you find yourself stuck and need some inspiration.

Clients Love Rules

I remember when I first realised the importance of rules for my business. I suppose we all have implicit rules in our business, but this was about making those rules explicit. On the instructions of my mentor, I sat down to really think about them.

My mind went blank. Completely blank. All I could come up with was "no dickheads".

Easy-peasy, I thought, I've got this nailed.

Yeah, right. It's easy to say "no dickheads", but what does that mean in practical terms?

Seriously, though, you do need to think about how you want your business to be and how you work best. Think about what's important to you and why, and distil that thinking into a set of rules. You don't have to come up with the finished set of rules right away; they'll change as time passes, as you change and as your business changes. That's the beauty of using results to measure the success of your process of thoughts, beliefs, and actions: you have the freedom to change things you control and measure your results to determine the success of your process.

But it's not all about you. You also need to understand your clients *want* you to have rules. They want guidance and structure; they want to know what they need to do, when to do it, and how to do it. They want and need boundaries. As Dan Kennedy says, everyone is wandering around with an umbilical cord in their hands, looking for somewhere to plug it in.

I'm going to repeat that as it is VERY IMPORTANT.

Everyone is wandering around with an umbilical cord in their hands, looking for somewhere to plug it in.

Your sole purpose is to provide people with explicit instructions for plugging their umbilical cord into your business. And that needs rules because people like to follow rules. It gives them certainty and routine and makes them feel safe.

We're all looking for someone that makes things easier, with information we can understand, that "ahhh, and relax" feeling of having found the solution to our problem.

We often don't care what the solution *is*, only that we've found one that will work. People are looking for certainty and rules give us certainty—at least the certainty of experience, if not the outcome. Your rules say a lot about you, your values, and what a client can expect from you. They make your clients feel safe and comfortable. They tell your clients you've got this. You'll take care of them.

One of my rules revolves around being respectful of people's time. If I have a client who is consistently late, or cancels meetings at the last minute, or doesn't turn up, well, that's extremely disrespectful and impacts the good work I do for the rest of my clients. I had a client like that, for a short while. They were late for the first meeting, didn't respond in a timely manner to post-meeting questions and answers and then cancelled the second meeting with one minute to go. I'd spent an hour preparing for that cancelled meeting.

I didn't offer them a reschedule. I politely informed them I could not help them with their problem. In other words, I fired them.

How many of this sort of client do you bend over backwards for because you don't have unequivocal rules?

How you implement your rules also says a lot about you. With the clients above, I could have become shirty with them, been judgmental, or critical. Instead, I took personal responsibility for not adequately confirming they were still okay for the meeting an hour before. Sure, a cancellation would still have been frustrating, but I wouldn't have wasted an hour on preparations.

I now have systems and processes in place to avoid the risk of clients cancelling very late or just not turning up (Calendly again!) And if they still do mess me around, well, it's au revoir.

Clearly there are extenuating circumstances sometimes because life happens, so there is understanding and flexibility, but you're not a contortionist (or maybe you are!) so flex, don't bend. It's your business, your rules.

Whilst rules provide the structure, they also help demonstrate your values as long as they're relevant. You might not want to work with clients who drive a Range Rover, for whatever reason—but that's not relevant unless you run an eco-friendly car fuel business!

Keep your rules relevant and keep them simple. And explain why they're there.

What's Next?

Remember, rules give you control over your business, so your business supports your life—not the other way around.

It's okay to set rules for your clients; in fact, rules make clients feel happier and more secure. You know this if you think about it: what businesses do you most enjoy working with? I bet it's the ones who have clear boundaries in place. You always know where you are with them.

So, set some rules of your own:

1. Note down your biggest business frustration: what causes you the most stress?
2. Write down what your life would be like without that source of stress and frustration.
3. How can you remove or mitigate it? Turn that solution into a rule and start implementing it today.

8

VALUE AND WORTH

IF YOU DON'T VALUE YOURSELF, HOW DO YOU
EXPECT ANYONE ELSE TO VALUE YOU?

W hen I talk to clients about pricing, there is one thing
that shines through: fear. Fear of failure. Fear of
rejection. Fear of other people's opinions.

Go back to Chapter 4 on your state of being. If your
thoughts are grounded in what you imagine other people to be
thinking about your prices, then you are guessing. You do not
know what other people are thinking. None of us do. By all
means ask them, but that won't help much as most people
don't say what they mean, anyway. They typically say what
they think you want to hear.

So, let's get the key message out there right from the start:
You do not have the right to decide what your clients are
willing to pay. Nor do you have the right to decide what value
they get from your products and services. You only have the
right to decide the value *you* place on your worth and thus the
prices *you* decide to charge.

Controversial. But what does it mean?

You have no right to decide what your clients are willing or
able to pay because you don't know how much they can
afford, and they won't tell you. You also don't know how
valuable your product or service is to them. How many times

have you thought, "I don't think they'll pay that" and then the client pays happily?

I've done it often over the years. We're imagining. Projecting. Unless we know what our widget is worth to our client, then we have absolutely no idea what value our clients place on our services.

Sometimes, by the way, we can work out exactly what our services are worth to our clients, in time and money, at any rate. A business owner I know quoted for a client with an asbestos problem. The client needed to reroute a stack of pipework at a known cost of £30,000—or they could remove the asbestos problem altogether. Removing the problem was actually quite easy and a specialist contractor could do it in a couple of days at a cost of £10,000. My client charged £25,000 for the work. Why? Because the value to the end client was a £5,000 saving on the alternative. He'd identified the value of his worth and priced accordingly.

And that's without factoring in unquantifiable value, like stress and mess and peace of mind.

If you price based on what you *think* a client will pay, you are projecting. If you price on what you *think* is your industry norm, you are projecting. You're projecting your own limiting beliefs onto others and imagining what your client is thinking. You have no idea what they're thinking so stop guessing.

"But my industry is different, Nick. I can't charge higher prices."

No, your industry isn't different. And yes, you can. Your pricing decision is on you.

You don't know what your client is willing or able to pay, so set your price according to how much profit you want to make; decide your worth. Now, there is some "elasticity" to pricing, meaning there comes a point where sales will drop off markedly because the price is too high. So, do some tests. Increase your prices by 10% right now and see what happens. I bet all that happens is you make more profit.

Then increase your prices again and again until you find the sweet spot, assuming you remain comfortable that you are continuing to offer value for money. Sure, you may lose a few clients, but they're the ones who don't appreciate your value or who can't afford to pay. The ones who stay are paying more and appreciate your value. Their investment is higher, which usually means they are less hassle and easier to work with. You'll also be making more profit. Less is sometimes more.

Remember, this is about thoughts, beliefs, and actions leading to results, the measure of the success of your process. In this case, the process is your pricing. You think you are worth £x and you believe that to be true. You take action to price according to the value you believe you are worth, then you measure the results. The results tell you how successful your process to establish your worth is.

But What About Price Resistance?

You'll always find someone who refuses to pay the advertised price based on some misguided principle. It has nothing to do with value; they just think they're special and shouldn't have to pay full price. Or they simply don't believe in ever paying full price for anything. These people aren't special and you don't have to work with them. You're doing a disservice to your valued clients when you let a discounting client in. Why should they pay less?

And what does that say about the true value of your services if you offer discounts to everyone who asks for one?

If these discount hunters want more for less now, what will they be like in six months or six years' time? If they don't value your worth now, what challenges will you face with them later?

I remember having this conversation with a prospective client. I demonstrated how he could make significant tax savings in the multi-hundreds of thousands of pounds. The value was clear, but the chap fixated on the cost of the advice rather than the value and quality of the advice—and the results the advice would bring him.

I explained that if he would like my advice to cost less, I could certainly remove elements of the solution for him—but that will of course mean the tax savings are commensurately reduced. He wanted more value for less investment.

But he's not paying for a piece of information in my head; he's paying for my years of experience, the exams I had to do, the knowledge I have gained, and the time I've spent developing a solution especially for him, to help him save a great deal of money.

If he wants the savings I can provide for him he has to pay my fee. I can phase the solution over time to spread the cost, or I can dispense with some elements entirely—but my price is my price. It fairly reflects the value, the quality, and the service excellence I deliver.

I haven't heard from him since, and I haven't chased him. I don't want price-sensitive clients. That's one of my rules. I'm looking for quality and service-sensitive clients, people who understand and respect the importance of high-quality advice and service excellence, and are happy to invest in it.

Small Changes Create Big Profits

How do you decide your price?

There are plenty of textbooks on pricing strategies, so if you really want to get into economic and behavioural theory, fill your boots. In this book, we don't need a bunch of theories because you're just going to put your prices up and measure the results until you find what works for you. Keep it simple.

However, you do need to understand your numbers and understand how and why a small increase in price has a large effect on profit.

To do this, you need to know your fixed costs and your variable costs.

Fixed costs are the costs you pay even if you sell nothing for a month. Like your office rent, staff salaries, pensions, insurance, vehicles, heat, light, software licenses. Variable costs are those that you incur only when you sell something. Like buying the parts to make the stuff you sell, or fuel for the van.

Let's say your variable cost for making each widget is £10. That includes materials, labour, and utilities. Now let's say your business's fixed costs are £5,000 a month. (That's £60,000 a year.) If you sell your widgets for £20 each, then you need to sell 500 widgets a month to break even, giving you no profit. Five hundred widgets a month provides just enough profit above the cost of making your widget to cover all your fixed costs for the year.

Now let's look to your personal costs. Essential costs are things you can't turn off, like your mortgage or rent, utility bills (gas, water, electricity), life insurance and food. You must still spend on these things even if you stop spending everywhere else you can.

Discretionary spending is money you could save if you really had to. Like holidays, clothes, and eating out.

Add the essential and discretionary expenditure together, including any savings you need to make to fund kids at University or your retirement, and work out how much that is every year. Let's say your total personal costs are also £60,000 a year, or £5,000 per month.

You now need to sell a further 500 widgets each month to break even in the business *and* make enough profit to meet your personal expenses. That's 1,000 widgets a month now.

Don't forget tax though. HMRC wants its share of your hard-earned cash. There are too many combinations of business and personal tax that may affect you and your business to work out those costs here. Make sure you get professional tax advice so you know exactly how to work out your tax liability each year. However, we'll ignore tax for now and keep this demonstration simple.

So, you need to sell 1,000 widgets a month to cover the costs of the business and meet your personal expenses, ignoring taxation.

What would happen if you put your widget price up by 10% to £22?

Well, assuming you sell the same number of widgets, you'll make an extra £2 per widget. And if you sell 1,000 widgets a month, you'll make an extra £2,000 a month (ignoring tax for ease).

Which means your profits, after paying all fixed business costs, have gone from £60,000 per year to £84,000. That's an extra £24,000 per year before taxes.

"Hold on, that's over 10% Nick!" Yep, you're absolutely right. Amazing, isn't it? A small increase in price has a tremendous impact on profit.

In this example, increasing the price by 10% adds 40% to the profit. Your numbers will be different and will lead to a different result, so please take professional advice before putting your prices up.

As you already know, if you want to measure the success of your process you need to measure the result, which is why it is crucial that you do the work to understand your business numbers before you do anything else.

You might worry about losing clients if you put your prices up by 10%. Firstly, you'll lose fewer clients than you think. And many of them won't even notice the slight price increase.

But if you do lose some, how many could you afford to lose if you put your price up by 10%? How much do you need to still cover all your personal expenses?

The business still needs to cover its costs of £5,000 a month and it needs to make a profit of £5,000 a month to cover your personal expenses. Your business needs to bring in £10,000 a month, minimum.

Your widgets now cost £22 each and cost you £10 each to make, so that's £12 profit per widget. This means you only need to sell 834 widgets (instead of 1,000) to meet all your costs. That's weird. That's 17% fewer widgets sold to make the same profit.

In this example, if you put your price up by 10%, you can afford to lose nearly 17% of your sales and *still* make the same money. Or, more likely, you'll make nearly 40% more profit as you'll probably keep most of your clients.

So, what are you going to do now? Are you going to worry about the opinions of others, or put your prices up and measure the result?

Of course, you may already be a premium seller and your pricing may already be at or close to the sweet spot. In which case, it's quite possible that the result will be negative. That's okay though, because you've learned something valuable: you've learned that you're at the sweet spot on price for that product or service.

Don't forget to split-test your pricing. Test a price increase with a handful of clients and measure the result. Roll it out gradually, using the tests to measure the success of your process. Did you find that one way of telling people about the increase had a better result than another way? Great. Take that message and split-test it again. Continuously refine your process as you continue to test, tweaking as you go and measuring results with your numbers.

Are you still pondering? Worried you'll be more expensive than the industry "going rate" and nobody will buy from you? Nonsense. Do not worry.

There is no such thing as an industry rate; there's just the average of everybody else's rates. Your industry is made up of many prices and pricing strategies. You know people who charge less than you for the same or very similar widgets or services. Perhaps you feel pressured into dropping your prices, to keep up (or down) with them. Don't. These businesses are so desperate for work they'll price jobs with no profit, or sometimes to take a loss, in the mistaken belief that it will lead to more work.

This sort of pricing strategy does significant damage to everybody: it's a race to the bottom nobody can win.

Maybe you also know people who charge more than you, and you wonder how they get away with it—and believe you couldn't possibly charge that much. Don't make excuses to yourself like, "They don't do the same thing." That's just more BS. If your client is cold because their boiler is broken and it's snowing this week, they'll pay what you're asking to fix their boiler and get warm because what you're offering is of value to them. I'm not saying price-gouge and rip people off; just know your value and charge accordingly. Stuff the industry rate.

The day you conform to these accepted and wholly untrue norms is the day you admit you're just one of the crowd. The worst kind of business cowardice is conformity. The only competition you really have is yourself and the biggest thing standing in your way is your own limiting beliefs. People will pay, and pay well, to have their problems solved. Some people will be price sensitive, but we don't want those clients—so it doesn't matter what they think.

Think about the industry rate for a moment: it is just an average. Dodgy Den charges £50 per hour, Average Ann charges £70 an hour, and Top End Eddie charges £90 an hour. The average is £70 an hour; and that becomes the industry "going rate". Yet Eddie is charging 28.5% more than Ann. How can that be?

There will always be someone charging more than you. Look at Lidl and Waitrose. They both sell apples. I mean, an apple is an apple, right? But Waitrose charges more for it.

Why? Because people are buying the shopping experience, not just the apple.

Stop making excuses and start testing price changes. Make sure you monitor what's happening by knowing your numbers.

Avoid the Herd

Have you seen the picture of the line of sheep blindly following each other off a cliff?[1]

It's a silly visual representation of the herd mentality that says, "That's how my industry works." It's the blind following the blind: most businesses in your industry don't know much more about running a successful business than you do. And yet, everyone follows each other.

Eighty percent of the sheep (or people in your industry) do this—but you're better than that.

Conformity is your enemy here. The more you conform to what everyone else is doing, the more you homogenise your service so it becomes the same as everyone else's. If you don't stand out, people will have no way to decide between you—and they will decide on price. If you're not the cheapest, you lose.

By doing the same thing everyone else does, you'll get the same results as everyone else. Think differently. Be different. Do something different. Put your prices up. Set your own rules and boundaries and stick to them.

If you want to stand out from the crowd, demonstrate your value, and run a brilliant business with great clients and the profits you want, then for goodness' sake, do the right thing. Stop following the crowd and instead define your business your way. Set boundaries, communicate them, and live by them. Your clients will respect you for it. Those clients, because they respect you and are investing money and time into working with you, are a pleasure to work with. They understand and appreciate your value and happily refer you to other customers just like them. All because you are clear about your rules and because you stand out from everyone else in your industry as something special: worth the extra investment.

The moment you enter the social media echo chamber, though, and start following the crowd, you're heading into oblivion. You join and perpetuate the race to the bottom on price *and* quality. You turn your product or service into a commodity that is traded on price, because you look exactly the same as everyone else. This makes it easy for clients to compare you to the alternative and thus price becomes your only differentiator. There will always be some idiot who does what you do for pennies. Let's make sure it isn't you.

Being contrary, not following the herd, means watching what the crowd is doing, then doing the opposite—or at least look for a different way. Be different so you can stand out and position yourself as the expert.

If you're wondering how to do this, here's a simple place to start. Your industry will probably have its negative stereotypes, characterised by a set of collective behaviours, real or perceived. Think: cowboy builders, dodgy tarmac contractors, life coaches who've only been on the National Express coach to London, LinkedIn gurus who think likes, views, comments, and shares are the measure of success. (It isn't. When it comes to marketing, sales and happy clients are the only measure of success.)

If you want to stand out, be contrary. Do something different. Starting with taking a stand against the thing people hate most about your industry. That will get you noticed by the right type of clients.

What's Next?

Remember, you have no right to decide how much someone will pay for your services, or how much value they get from it. But you can decide to deliver an amazing product or service and charge accordingly.

1. Start by putting your prices up by 10%—and watch your profits increase instantly.
2. Get a grip on your numbers: what are your fixed and variable costs? How much are your personal expenses each month? What do you need to bring in to cover everything? How does taxation affect the result?
3. Decide how much profit you want to make after you've covered all your expenses—then figure out how you're going to make that happen.

9

THE DARK ART

MARKETING IS NOT A DIRTY WORD

There's an enduring idea that marketing is a Dark Art. That it's mucky, manipulative, and we shouldn't have to get our hands dirty.

That's not true. Marketing is simply this: solving people's problems and helping them get what they want.

More than that: without marketing, you don't have a business. So let's look at the Dark Art.

Firstly, though, I am not a marketing expert. I am not a copywriter. I am not a designer. I am not a direct response guru. But I am an experienced business owner and I've seen for myself what works to bring in new clients—and what doesn't work. I also have a mentor who is an expert on this stuff, and he in turn is mentored by one of the world's foremost marketing experts.

I will not tell you what to do here, nor am I seeking to teach you all about marketing—but I do hope to open your eyes to some rubbish that gets spouted by marketers and designers regularly. Be careful what you listen to or you'll end up spending vast amounts of money to massage your ego.

Let's start with "why".

"People don't buy what you do, they buy why you do it"

If you haven't seen it, Google Simon Sinek's TED Talk about: "People don't buy what you do." It is absolutely fascinating, and it will change your perspective on your business and your marketing.

Simon talks about how most businesses know *what* they do. We make widgets; we sell financial products; we sell furniture.

Some businesses know *how* they do it. They might call it their value proposition or their unique selling point. We're not talking about the physical manufacturing process for a product here; we're talking about what makes them different from other people doing the same thing.

But very few businesses understand *why* they do what they do. We're not talking about the economic why of profit or shareholder value; that is just the result of doing business. We're talking about the organisational purpose: why the business exists, the cause or the problem it is trying to solve.

It's the answer to the question, "Why do you get out of the bed in the morning, and why should anyone care?"

As business owners, we typically communicate *what* we do because we have a clear and comprehensive understanding of it. We're passionate about our product or service. We're highly qualified in our technical area and we love nothing more than talking about it. At networking events, people talk about what they do as if it defines them.

"What do you do Nick?"

"I'm a financial consultant."

We think in terms of *what*, but clients buy in terms of *why*. The truly smart business owner understands this, and sells their Why, not their What.

I'll use Simon Sinek's Apple example as it's easy to understand and we can all relate to it. If Apple were like most business owners, they'd talk like this: "We make great computers (the What), they're beautifully designed, simple to use, and user friendly (the How), want to buy one?"

If you look back at early Apple marketing, this is exactly how they communicated. They listed specifications, features, and benefits—and expected people to buy. This might have appealed to the nerdy computer geek, but it didn't create mass-market appeal.

This is how most business owners communicate.

Think about networking events and how people introduce themselves. They start by giving their job or business title, their business name, and a list of products or services, before then asking for business or referrals.

For example: "Hi, I'm Nick Smith from Somerset Wealth Management. I'm a financial consultant and I specialise in investments and retirement planning for business owners. If you'd like to know more, please get in touch." (Watch as people bomb-burst to all four corners of the room!)

I've never actually said the above, but I would reprimand myself sharply if I did, because nobody gives a shit about what I do or how I do it. Prospective clients care only about whether I can solve their problem. They care about their problem and whether it is a match with my Why.

Nobody really wakes up in the morning and thinks, "I'd really like to get a pension today." They might say, "I'm worried about whether I'll ever be able to retire," though, which is a different question requiring a different approach to marketing.

Here's how Apple communicates today: "In everything we do, we believe in challenging the status quo. We believe in thinking differently. The way we challenge the status quo is by making our products beautifully designed, simple to use, and user friendly. We just happen to make great computers. Want to buy one?"

"People don't buy what you do, they buy why you do it."

If you communicate with lists of features and benefits,

you're telling people what you do, and they just don't care. Apple's marketing creates a feeling inside you. They create an emotional response in our brains by starting their message with their why—something we can emotionally connect with.

How many times have you heard or said, "I understand all the facts and figures, I can see all the features and benefits, but it just doesn't feel right."

This is because the part of our brain that controls decision-making is emotional. The part of our brain that understands facts and figures doesn't make decisions. We buy through our emotions, then rationalise our decisions later using those facts and figures. Focusing on your why taps into that emotional inner core of your client's mind.

The Dark Art

Marketing, to me, is a black art—or so I thought. I hated it. The terminology, the confusing information, the sales pitches about reach, conversion, lead generation, and opportunities, all of which felt, to me, like they were distilling the very essence of building long-term relationships with clients into cold categories and numbers on a page.

Everyone I spoke to had a different opinion and none of them seemed to add up. Some said sponsorship was the best way. Get involved with a local club or organisation and use sponsorship to raise your profile. Others banged the drum for advertising: raise awareness of what you do through local publications (note they used the term "what you do"). Others recommended direct mail: buy a list of targeted prospects who are already interested in buying from you (are they?) Or how about Facebook Ads: put ads in front of people who've just mentioned "retirement" in a post.

None of it made any sense to me. I'd try one of them and sort of hope for the best, not really knowing what I was doing —and surprise, surprise, it rarely met any of the expectations set by the salesperson. I'm sure there are plenty of examples of each of those marketing tactics working very effectively, but I've realised that you need an expert to make it happen. I am not a marketeer so trying to DIY my marketing would never work.

I know, I know. I'm lecturing on the use of experts and ignored my own advice. Busman's holiday.

At the same time as wallowing around with no clear idea about marketing, I met an accountant who told me about his mentor, the Evil Bald Genius, aka Jon McCulloch—an expert in marketing, positioning, pricing, and business mindset. Now, he's not everyone's cup of tea (Marmite springs to mind) but he really knows his eggs from his bacon when it comes to the stuff I hated: marketing. I took the plunge and applied to join Jon's Elite Mastermind Group. I knew I needed help in a number of areas, not just one, and I saw the value in getting this stuff right. I never looked back.

I also love marmite. You're properly weird if you don't.

I quickly realised that 90% of success in business comes from our mindset. With the right attitude, we can achieve almost anything, hence why this book talks a great deal about mindset. The same principles apply to financial management as they do to business management. Get the mindset right and everything else will follow.

The Flagpole Effect

It was around that time I also realised I am, in fact, a marketeer. Like it or not. I'm not in the financial consultancy business; I'm in the marketing of financial consultancy business.

The reality is, I'm not selling widgets by the million impersonally, having no contact with the end consumer. I'm nurturing a long-term relationship to help people discover the secret wealth inside their business and navigate their way to affluent prosperity. It's a personal relationship, and that means I have to market *me*. Not financial products, but me, the person. Because people buy from people and my clients need to know they can trust me to do the right thing.

Only last week I was talking to a prospective new client and his son. The client is an elderly gentleman with substantial cash savings. Their expectation was that I would recommend investing a significant proportion of the cash savings rather than leaving it in cash. I did the opposite. I recommended leaving the cash in cash, but spreading it around a bit to benefit from government protection.

Why? Because my elderly client didn't need to take any investment risk. His primary objective was to ensure he had enough to pay his bills and meet any future care needs without having to do a fire-sale of the house.

Sure, his kids might like to invest some of it for growth for their future benefit, but I wasn't advising the kids.

As I write this, we're in our first COVID winter and given my client's low appetite for risk, investment solutions just didn't fit.

Why am I telling you this? To demonstrate that doing the right thing is a core value and that doing the right thing is my Why. They were surprised and grateful. They were expecting to feel pushed into investing (from which I would obviously make a fee). What they actually got was an honest assessment of their circumstances and a recommendation that was right for them.

That honesty has done more for building trust in our relationship than any brochure, leaflet, banner, or flagpole in the car park.

Marketing doesn't have to be expensive. You don't have to spend oodles of money listing product features that no-one cares about in the local rag. You don't have to "invest" in banners and event sponsorship for your local footy team except to massage your own ego. By all means, go ahead if you feel the need to show everyone how you've made it with a bunch of banners, flags, and adverts. Your clients don't care about your flagpole in the staff car park; they just want their problem fixed.

Social Media

What about social media? Google Ads, Facebook Ads, LinkedIn Marketing, Twitter? TikTok? There'll be a bunch of new ones by the time I publish this.

The problem is, social media is an echo chamber. We watch, read, like, and comment on posts that resonate with us (unless you're a troll). We connect with people who are like us. We skip past stuff we don't like or disagree with.

The social media algorithms know what we're doing. They know how long we paused on that video, how much of it we watched, how slowly or quickly we scrolled. The algorithms learn what we read, comment, and follow and feed us more of the same to keep us hooked, to keep us online so we see more adverts. The more we interact with certain content styles, the more of that style we see.

Social media echoes back what we do on their platform. It feeds itself.

It's the same with online adverts. You must have noticed how the adverts you see always seem to relate to the searches you've made recently. Spent last night looking for holidays in Mallorca? That's funny, I've seen two ads for holidays in Mallorca on my Facebook feed this morning.

Social media echoes back the views we support and express. We will continue to see more and more of the same. This is no bad thing, because it helps us build a network of like-minded people. Because they like you, they like your content, and they like what you say and do, then you have a pool of potential prospects with a higher likelihood of buying from you.

The problem occurs when you're not yourself, when you don't say what you really mean, when you don't act in a way that is congruent with who you are. Are you afraid of judgement, criticism, and trolls on social media? Get over it, because it's going to happen. Do you temper your words, soften them so as not to offend anyone? Do you avoid confrontational posts and conversations? Do you fear rejection? Do you seek approval? Do you worry that what you say and how you say it will put some potential clients off?

Well, I've got news for you: that's exactly what you want to do. That might sound like a risky strategy, but it's not: I only want to work with clients who are like me. I'm not saying you should deliberately be offensive to create a reaction, but be yourself. Use the echo chamber to filter out unsuitable clients and attract people you'll love working with. Remember, offence can only be taken, not given.

We cannot please everyone, so don't try. It's far better to have ten evangelical clients who will pay your prices because they value the work you do, than 100 clients, some of whom you perhaps don't like, who are demanding, and who push you down on price.

I recall commenting on a LinkedIn post about being "authentic", which is the new mindset buzzword doing the rounds. I commented that my wife calls me "stable, dependable, reliable... and [fucking] boring." It's a bit tongue-in-cheek, but it's a fair reflection of who we are as a couple and our sense of fun together. Another LinkedIn user questioned whether it was wise to say such a thing on social media, as people might interpret it in ways I didn't intend. She said I'd be better off trying to attract clients by writing about positive traits that potential clients would find attractive.

The thing is, how the hell do I (or anyone else) know what a client finds attractive? If I imagine what a client will find attractive and write for that, I will attract clients who are attracted to words that aren't me! That'll never be a good fit.

The funny thing is, many of these so-called authentic people come across as inauthentic and egotistical. It's not deliberate; it's just they don't actually know who they are yet. They haven't taken the time to truly understand their own mind and to work on their mindset, so their authenticity can come across as incongruent and inconsistent. This doesn't mean they are being inauthentic; it just means they need to do more work on themselves. This is not a universal truth of course, just my opinion.

Of course, perhaps their approach is successful as it is repelling me, and we wouldn't be a good fit. That may be true; I'm just not convinced they know that's what they're doing.

The purpose of your social media strategy is to attract the 10 evangelical clients and repel the 100 unsuitable ones. You need to do both, or you'll waste vast amounts of time weeding out the good from the bad.

For example, I don't enjoy working with those who have an extreme left-wing political bent. I work hard, take risks and pay my taxes. I am rewarded for this in the success of my business. If you remove or stifle the reward, you stifle innovation. I have other rules, too, as you'll have seen throughout this book—and you'll no doubt have your own. Rules like this are important because it stops you taking on the wrong clients. And when we talk about our rules—our values —it helps us attract the kinds of clients who we'll get on with, and who we'll be able to get the best results for, all while gently repelling those we don't want to work with.

The Reluctant Marketer

I've gone from seeing marketing as a dark art to having a much better understanding of the relative merits of different marketing avenues and how they work. I remain a reluctant marketeer, but I have the support and accountability I need to grow my business and attract the right clients at the right price. That has come at a price. A pounds and pence price because expertise isn't free, but it is invaluable to get me where I want to be.

Whenever I think about my marketing messages, which is every time I put pen to paper, finger to keyboard, or words in my mouth, I remember two things from my marketing journey: Simon Sinek's talk on the importance of why, and that clients buy fixes for their problems. Most of my clients genuinely don't give two hoots about how pension tax relief works! They care only that I can help them build a pension fund that will enable them to have the retirement they dream of.

Your responsibility as a business owner is to understand your client's problem inside out, back to front, and be able to solve it in your sleep. It helps if you've also experienced the same problem too. I certainly did when I used the services of financial advisers in the past. I was never satisfied with the service or the outcome. They never convinced me they genuinely understood what I wanted and needed, or the problem I felt inside me. They didn't seem to connect with my emotional need for empathy and understanding about my money future.

So I set up on my own. I wanted to build a business where the client experience was core, even if that meant I was rapidly paddling my feet in the background. I don't always get it right because I'm a human being, as are my team—but we work damn hard to make the client experience slick and pleasant, within the realms of what we can control. In the same way as I give empathy and understanding to my clients, I look for the same in return.

I have moved from the dark arts to apprentice magician, reluctantly. I understand marketing and how it works much better now. I understand where marketing fits into my process. I understand the need for numbers to measure the success of my marketing process. And I understand the success of marketing is derived from a successful, repeatable process. It is not a single event; it's an ongoing strategy with different tactics used in different ways at different times

What's Next?

Get comfortable with marketing! It's the only way you'll bring in the right customers and clients—or any customers and clients.

Start with your ideal client:

1. What's the fundamental problem you're solving for them, in their eyes?
2. What pain is it causing them and why?
3. Armed with this knowledge, how can you find them?

10

AUTOMATION AND SYSTEMATISATION
THE KEYS TO AN EASY LIFE

Y our account has been locked due to multiple failed login attempts. Please contact customer support." (For which it is virtually impossible to find a telephone number).

"Your password must contain the following." (Why didn't you tell me that before I put the password in? You've now emptied the form so I have to start all over again!)

"If we hold an account with that email address, you will receive a password reset email." (Where the hell is it then?)

I can understand why we get increasingly frustrated with the technology we use because whilst it might be functionally correct and much of it improves life, the daily user experience can be very poor.

The fact the form emptied because your password didn't contain a capital letter isn't wrong, but it is immensely frustrating to the user. This happens because of poor design: the individual components of the system work as they should, but when put together they fail to deliver a seamless experience. I've seen so much of this in my career.

After I left the Royal Navy, I became a project and programme manager, initially in IT, then later in large-scale business and IT change programmes in financial services. The process for creating a new system or changing an existing one is broadly similar in every industry. The scale of it may be different, but the principles remain the same.

The great promise of the 1980s was that computers would change the world by improving our lives, by making things easier to do. To a large extent that has happened. If we think about how computing technology has contributed to huge advances in medical science, aviation safety, or the detection of serious crime, then yes, technology has without doubt contributed to positive improvements for society and our lives.

But is it really *easier* now, or is it just different?

Ultimately, computers, systems, and technology are designed by people and people remain the weakest link in any chain because we make mistakes. We are human. The more complex the system, the harder it is to design, build, maintain, and consistently deliver on client expectations. And the more likely it is that flaws will creep in.

Tech is Here to Stay

Technology is here to stay and if you're going to achieve personal sovereignty and affluent prosperity, then you need to embrace what technology can do for you.

"But Nick, my business is a people business, it's all about my personal relationship with my client. I can't automate my client meetings."

Indeed, and I'm not suggesting you do—but the mere fact you have client meetings (plural) means you are doing something repeatable. And if you are doing something repeatable, then you (should) have a system to ensure consistency and accuracy. That doesn't mean you have to automate it with a computer, but do have a repeatable and consistent process, a system.

Let's say you run a website design business. You know exactly what outcome you want from your client meeting so you can design and build their website; you have a client engagement process; a system. If you stop and think about your client meetings, I bet they follow a consistent and repeatable process: introductions, a bit about your website design experience, a high-level understanding of what your client is looking for and why, detailed discussions about the number of pages they want, and search engine optimisation. This is your process and you need to document it.

"Seriously, why do I need to document what I do? I've been doing it for years, I know exactly what I'm doing and it works." Okay, but you're either not being honest with yourself or you have something semi-documented already. Perhaps you have a wee checklist that you use (that's a process) or a high-level agenda that prompts you (that's a process too), or it's ingrained in your head. Either way, there's a process you follow—but if you don't write it down, you won't *see* the opportunities to refine and improve it, which may include systematisation and potentially automation.

Remember, this book is all about your personal sovereignty and affluent prosperity: how to find sustainable wealth, a richer lifestyle, and an enduring legacy with less financial hassle. Until you remove some of yourself (your time) from the processes in your business, you won't make much headway with sovereignty. To make your processes more efficient, you need to understand what you do, and how that equates to your time and energy.

I started with a large roll of brown paper laid across a table (stuck on a wall is equally good), piles of multi-coloured sticky notes and several thick-ish Sharpie pens. The first thing I did was think about one element of my business and write down all its components. I wrote each element of my client onboarding process on a sticky note, using different colours for different components. For example, I was blue, clients were yellow, documents were white, and computer stuff was red— but you'll find your own method that works for you.

There was no organisation at this point. I just wrote each aspect as I thought about it, then stuck the post-it onto the paper in no particular order. You end up with a disorganised dump of everything that happens in that process. Well, I say "everything": you'll find large elements missing, which we'll come to later.

Step two: order your thoughts by putting the sticky notes in some kind of order or process flow. For example, you might start with a sticky note that says "new client emails to make an appointment" in the top left, followed by "arrange meeting by email," then "confirm directions to client's office," and "confirm meeting 24 hours before."

You may have started with "arrange meeting" but when you give it further thought, you see that "arrange meeting" contains multiple components. Now, leave it for a few days and come back to it because you will see it differently with fresh eyes.

At some point, you'll need to tidy up your sticky notes and brown paper. There are so many software options for this so choose the one that's right for you. I suggest you don't use a word processor because you'll struggle to see the entire process.

What you really need is a flowchart. Software like Visio or LucidChart will help you create one. Transfer your sticky notes onto a flowchart so you can see what you do and how each element of your process flows and interacts. The advantage of moving to a software flowchart is when you want to make a change, add in a process or remove one, it's much easier than trying to shuffle all your post-it notes around to accommodate the change.

This isn't easy, by the way. It will challenge you to really think about what you do and to break the constituent parts into as much (reasonable) detail as possible so you can see what's missing, and what you can improve.

Having done your flowchart, you now have a system, a

repeatable process that describes what you do—but it doesn't address *how* you do it and that's important. Don't get into the detail of "how" just yet. That comes later.

Systematising Your Process

Whilst a flowchart is a great start to refining your process, you can't use it to manage delivery of your consistent process. Instead, it acts as a pictorial view of what you do. Now, you need to systematise what you do into how you do it.

Take that flowchart and turn it into the process steps you and your team need to take every time you bring on a new client. Again, there are plenty of software options here so find the one that works best for you. Do a little research with your team (if you have a team).

Here are a few places to look: ClickUp, Trello, Process Street, Monday.com. I can't possibly show or tell you how to set up your business processes. That will depend on you and your business. But I can give you an example of a consistent process I use to get information about a client's existing investments held elsewhere.

It sounds simple, but unless it's rigorously managed, I quickly find myself in a right pickle, not knowing what information I've asked of whom and when. Here's how I do it:

1. Determine if provider accepts electronic letters —check **CRM**
2. If provider is new, call provider and add details to **CRM**
3. Send authority letter and cover letter
4. Update **CRM** with date and method sent (post or email)
5. In 3 days, call provider, check letter received and get commitment about when they'll respond

6. Update CRM with expected date of response and include any other call notes
7. Confirm response received by committed date
8. If not, chase provider and update CRM
9. On receipt, scan and file response in client file
10. Raise action to review data response

There are many more steps in this process and you don't need to know them all to understand the point. What started out as a post-it note on a roll of brown paper that just said "send letter of authority" has turned into a multi-step detailed process that any member of staff can follow without making errors.

This is important. Remember, we're trying to find sustainable wealth, a richer lifestyle, and an enduring legacy. By drilling down into your processes, systematising and understanding them, you will identify opportunities for automation and opportunities for delegation without detriment to your client experience.

In fact, it's very likely you will improve your client experience as your process will ensure nothing gets missed, forgotten, or delayed.

What we have now is a detailed set of repeatable manual tasks in an off-the-shelf software system. With the right software, you'll be able to save these repeatable tasks as a template so every time a new client comes along, you can "apply" the template to create the same repeatable list of tasks.

Because you're using software, you can also see where you are with all the repeatable tasks. Taking my example above, I can now see, at a glance, how many letters I have in process across all providers and clients, and where they are. I can see, at a glance which providers I must call this week for further information, so my staff only make one call to gather information for multiple clients and/or multiple investments.

This saves time. This saves money. This is less hassle than trying to remember what was where.

This is a step on the road to personal sovereignty. It vastly reduces error rates and allows me to be really effective at managing my time and my team's time. It is highly efficient: as much of the process as possible is automated, and the manual tasks are all scheduled and easy to do.

Automating Your Process

Taking one step at a time, you can start automating and enriching your manual repeatable tasks in the software to save even more time, create even more consistency, and increase efficiency. Stop and think about every single step in the process and ask how you could improve the automation of that step.

Now, when I talk about automation, I mean two things. One, how you can automate the creation of a task based on a previous task or action. And two, how you can automate a manual task (so it's not done by you).

They are very different things.

We can improve and enrich the template by adding further detail to each task. We can assign a specific team member to a task and add a time estimate so when we apply the template, we don't have to do it manually and the task automatically appears in that team member's to-do list with a correct due date.

You can build software automations that decide whether a task even appears by using logic statements such as "if response not received by committed date then add task to chase provider in 24 hours. Assign task to X with a time estimate of 30 minutes (we spend a lot of time on hold in this business!), set the due date for tomorrow, and priority as high." This stops unnecessary tasks appearing at all and improves efficiency.

You can ask your team to use the software's time tracker to

monitor how long they take to do each task, and you can then use this data to identify what your staff spend most of their time doing. With this data, you can identify where you need to invest your energy in automation to make your business more efficient.

Improving the process is a process in itself. In my software, I have a list of improvement ideas with a time estimate alongside them. Every week, I set aside time for process improvement and I use that prioritised list to make any improvements I can with the time I have allocated. If I don't finish something, it stays at a status of "in progress" and I work on it next week.

So, we've gone from post-it notes on brown paper, to a flowchart that describes what you do, to detailed repeatable task templates to reuse, to enriched tasks and automations that automatically assign tasks, set due dates and times, and create new tasks when you complete old tasks. This is all great stuff.

We've still only scratched the surface of how technology can help you achieve personal sovereignty because we've only really looked at what we can do inside one piece of software. The real joy of technology and the reason it's going to help you achieve personal sovereignty is the way we can connect different pieces of software together. We can get them talking to each other.

It's Good to Talk

Every business uses software somewhere; I have yet to come across one that thrives without it. You probably have multiple software systems that you and your staff use—possibly doubling up on work. Maybe you take data stored on one system and enter it onto another system.

For example, when you arrange a meeting with a prospective client, you have an email address and telephone number in your inbox somewhere. You have to get that into your contacts, your CRM, your Accounts system for invoicing, and/or your process or task management software. Someone has to type it in manually, and mistakes get made. Mistakes that disappoint clients, make it harder for clients to do business with you, and which cost time and money to rectify.

Imagine if your website directed clients to self-serve by booking a meeting directly into your calendar using Calendly, Acuity Scheduling, or similar. This means Calendly captures your client's name, email address, and telephone number. You can then easily build a connection between Calendly and your CRM that automatically creates a new client in your CRM when Calendly captures their information, which then automatically creates the new client onboarding template list of tasks. You don't have to touch it. It just happens.

This is what it looks like when systems talk to each other. At this level, it's very simple—and for many businesses, it's all they really need.

That might sound complicated, though, if you're not comfortable with technology. Some of this stuff sounds scary and difficult—but as with most things, it's only as scary as you tell yourself it is. As you say it, so it will become.

Don't worry if tech isn't your thing, because all you're going to do right now is what I've described above: you're going to get that roll of brown paper, sharpies, and post-it notes; you're going to build your flowcharts; you're going to choose your process and task management software; and you're going to write your lists of manual tasks. You should be able to do that fairly easily, because it's your business and you know it inside out.

The only other thing to add to your brown paper is a post-it note for each system you use. For each system, list the key items of data you use or need for your key business processes, like onboarding. For example, your CRM needs a name, email, date of birth, address, product or service, start date, end date, and price. Your accounts system needs some of that data, but not all of it. Your task management system may need product or service information. You may need (or want) to introduce electronic contract signatures with DocuSign.

DocuSign, by the way, is brilliant because you can integrate it with various systems that send the document, get it signed, and automatically add it back into the system. Imagine being able to select a task that says "send contract for signature", knowing that marking it as complete automatically sends a document for signature via DocuSign—and when signed, it automatically files it with the client record in your CRM and updates the contract start date. Brilliant.

Storytelling

You now have clear flowcharts, repeatable lists of manual tasks and a systems diagram that shows common data like name, email address, etc. So far, you haven't really had to step out of your comfort zone as everything you've listed is already in your head. The only new aspect is maybe the software you've chosen.

Now it's time to take your process and allocate each step or element to a system. Take your flowchart and colour-code each step according to which system the step happens on.

What you have then is a flowchart describing how you run your business, so you can instantly see the boundaries where your process moves from one system to another. These boundaries are ripe for automation. If step one is a client booking a meeting via Calendly and step two is adding client details to your CRM, you create a line from a step in Calendly's colour to a step in your CRM's colour.

This shows you exactly what you could streamline, where you could add an automation, and what it might look like.

An easy way to do this is with User Stories. Something like: "I want to add client details to my CRM and Accounting software when a new client books a meeting in Calendly."

I write all my improvement wish-list items as mini-stories that describe what I want to happen. It's usually something that will save the business time or reduce administration and error rates. I don't go into details about *how* the data will move between one system and another. This means I can quickly see what stories I've identified. I can see how important they are because I've given them a score. I can also see where we are in that process.

I'm quite techy because of my background, so I wrote and implemented most of my mini-stories myself—but I also worked with a developer for some more technical ones. I may be techy, but I don't pretend that I can write computer code and get it right. When it gets complicated or I'm short of time, I work with an expert to take one of my stories and make it happen. Because I've written the story in plain English, it's easy for him to understand and because I've made each one as small as I can make it, it doesn't get too complicated. Simplicity is key here.

If you don't have a techy background, though, this might all feel very overwhelming. So now's the time to find an automation consultant or developer to help you. This is an investment well worth making because a great developer or consultant will help you put systems in place that will save you enormous amounts of time and money. The investment should more than pay for itself within just a few months, or even weeks.

The more you can automate without making your systems too complicated, the more time you will have to spare, and the lower your error rates will be. Automation within your business will be key to achieving more time and personal sovereignty outside your business.

What's Next?

Start with your simplest process; I'd suggest the new client onboarding process:

1. Write all the elements of your process on post-its and stick them to the wall or a roll of brown paper. Use different colours or symbols to denote who does each one or where it happens, e.g. system, paper, Fred, Jane. The purpose is to see the entire process in one place, visually.
2. Arrange the post-its so they show the flow of what needs to happen, and in what order. Some items will happen at the same time and that's okay; just put the post-its right next to each other.
3. Now document that process for the whole team to follow so it's consistent.
4. Finally, give ownership of the process to one of your team, giving them authority to improve it as required.

11

THE FINANCIAL ACCELERATOR

HOW TO BUILD A SOLID FINANCIAL FOUNDATION

Nirvana does exist. It is entirely possible to find your own Nirvana and have it all. As long as we accept that fate will always have a hand, that there are things we can't control, and those things will often derail our efforts. Which is why we put plans in place to protect ourselves.

With every plan for affluent prosperity comes risk. The skilled financial consultant understands, articulates, and manages risk to give your financial and life plan the best possible chance of success; to make sure you stay on the rails despite everything life might throw at you. Most importantly, we write everything down to give you a place to start. I'd like you to create the best plan possible for you; however, any plan is better than no plan at all.

Imagine deciding to go on holiday, turning up at the airport, and getting on the plane. The pilots decided not to make a plan though. Instead, they just got in, started the engine, and took off. They knew they wanted to get to the Middle East, and they knew that was roughly south-east somewhere, so they headed off in that vague direction.

Ah, fuel, they need some fuel. How much have they got? Great, loads. Ah, but how far is it? Bugger—they don't know, and they don't really know where they're going. Dubai maybe? Oh well, let's keep heading in the rough direction of Dubai and hope they don't run out of fuel before they get somewhere.

That somewhere is pretty much guaranteed not to be Dubai.

This imaginary holiday scenario sounds pretty ridiculous, but I've just described most people's approach to affluent prosperity. They take off with no idea where they're going, no idea how much fuel they need (meaning how much money to invest) and no idea how long it will take to get to their destination (retirement)—if they even know what (and when) that destination is.

Most people just hope for the best. Never in human history has hoping for the best been a strategy for success. It's just being an ostrich.

And when it comes to your financial security and the future of your family, it's a crazy approach. We put more time and effort into planning our holidays than we do planning a secure financial future.

Why Put Off Until Tomorrow What You Can Do Today?

I understand why the thought of financial planning to grow your own destiny can feel daunting. It feels like a monumental task, so it's easy to put off until "tomorrow". I hold my hands up on behalf of my industry and take some responsibility for this: it's not entirely your fault. As an industry, much of the information presented to clients—to people like you—is frankly befuddling. There're reams and reams of repetitive paperwork, statistics and graphs, performance figures set over regulated intervals that bear no resemblance to client reality—and jargon.

There's stuffy static documentation from a single point in time that doesn't reflect the complexity and nuance of a dynamic plan for your future. You have to wade through financial "products" with names seemingly designed to confuse everyone: UFPLS—uncrystallised funds pension lump sum; PCLS—pension commencement lump sum; it's nonsense to everyone outside the financial services industry, and some on the inside too!

We write and talk in a language guaranteed to put every client off ever engaging in the financial planning process. I sometimes wonder if the industry does this on purpose to create an air of authority or superiority. Whether that's the aim or not, the result is advisers end up sitting on the other side of the table to their clients.

Why would we do that? We should all be sitting on the same side of the table with our clients, working together to do the right thing, at the right time, to get you one step closer to affluent prosperity.

We will not get there using obfuscating language and confusing terms to describe unnecessarily complex financial instruments. However, I'm unlikely to change this industry on my own, but it won't stop me trying!

A consequence of all this is: most financial advisers and consultants don't articulate a clear plan. They produce regulated documents that meet the FCA's static criteria for advice, dust off their hands, and say "job done." Meanwhile, the client has understood next-to-nothing about it.

It's almost as if the industry tries to put people off learning about their options.

The biggest problem is, most advisers are product-focused: they focus on conversations about life insurance, mortgages, pensions, and ISAs—all of which are the staple of the mainstream adviser.

I don't see financial advice like that.

Much like an airline pilot with their flight bag or a plumber with their tool bag, I keep a set of financial products in my tool bag which I may bring out to help you achieve your objectives.

But before we talk about any products, we're going to start with you: what you want, what you need, and where you are right now.

What's right for you today may not be right for you next year or the year after, so we'll change the tools we're using, if we need to.

The reality is, no-one wakes up in the morning and thinks to themselves, "Ooh, I'd really like a pension today." It's much more likely you're dreaming about what retirement could be; you want and need a retirement plan, but you don't know where to start.

So: where *do* we start?

The Financial Accelerator

Consider the idea of a three-legged stool. It can be a bit precarious; we've all sat down on a three-legged stool at some point and had it wobble—or even break. If one of those legs goes, everything comes tumbling down: the stool, and you. Each of those three legs needs to be solid if we want a safe, comfortable seat.

If one leg wobbles, you have two choices: ignore it, deal with the anxiety, and hope it won't eventually collapse under you (which it will); or fix it.

I use the three-legged stool analogy when thinking about affluent prosperity. A wobbly leg in your financial plan will one day bring everything crashing down to earth. If all three legs are strong and well balanced, your plan for affluent prosperity stays upright and solid.

You *might* get lucky and sail through life sitting on the wobbly stool that never fails… If that happens, you are truly blessed. Buy a lottery ticket. But why take the risk for no good reason? Hope is not an effective life strategy. Instead of trusting luck, take charge of your own financial future.

Sure, there's a small cost to fixing the stool and keeping it in good condition, but the security of knowing the stool won't break and plunge you into disaster far outweighs that little investment.

When it comes to achieving sustainable wealth, there are three core elements to manage:

- Risk
- Taxation
- Wealth

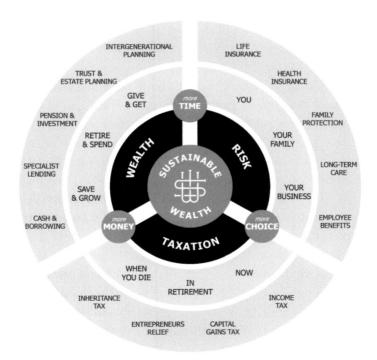

The Financial Accelerator Model

When your financial plan fully considers each element—risk, taxation, and wealth—when each leg is strong and balanced, the stool stays upright. If there's a wobbly leg, the stool totters and may fall.

Of course, even if the stool is sturdy, there's no guarantee everything will go to plan; a strong gust of wind (external factors) may unbalance you; or perhaps a misguided action on your part. But the stool will still be there for you to grab onto and haul yourself back up.

It remains a steady rock to anchor yourself. A sound plan for sustainable wealth.

The stool is your individual plan for the sustainable wealth element of affluent prosperity. The carpenter is me.

As a carpenter, I have a tree trunk and branches from which to make your stool. I don't start by sanding the leg or carving an intricate pattern into the branch and then try to make a leg from it. I start with the rough building blocks. I cut a large slice off the trunk, larger than I need to make the seat. I cut three good-sized branches to make the legs. Then I get the smaller tools out to refine and create the structure.

Later on, I'll sand and smooth, varnish and finesse, to create a masterpiece. It's not until some years later that your new stool takes on a beautifully weathered and crafted look.

It's the same with your sustainable wealth plan. We start with the building blocks. As time goes by we finesse the blocks to create a Picasso.

Before we do anything, you've decided where you're going, you've decided what you're trying to create, and we've sat down, thought about and defined your life and financial objectives. It's your plan, your stool; so it's your design. I can't decide those things for you, although I can guide your thinking and help draw it out of you.

I know that sounds difficult; I get it—which is why a good adviser helps you draw out your objectives and picture what's important to you and why. They'll work with you to understand your personal and business priorities, and help you translate them into tangible goals and objectives.

It's very much like coaching, really. It's all about asking the right questions, and searching for and teasing out the answers, which we often hold deep within. We challenge your assumptions and beliefs, motivate you, and hold you accountable for your part of the plan—and we keep you on track when you wobble or go astray.

Would you try to carve a stool from a tree without a plan? Would you fly to Dubai without a plan(e)? Would you seek your retirement dream without a financial plan? Hopefully not now you've read this far!

Despite all this, some people still don't want to listen. I understand that listening to and heeding expert advice isn't for everyone when you firmly believe you can already fly a plane.

If you do want to listen, though, read on. It's time to build your stool and make your plan for sustainable wealth.

What's Next?

Simple: decide to make a plan for your financial future. Then read the next chapters carefully.

I can help you—but you have to take the first step.

12

LET'S TALK ABOUT RISK

HOW MUCH ARE YOU WILLING TO RISK FOR SUSTAINABLE WEALTH?

W hat is risk?
  "This is."

The philosophy essay question on the Oxbridge entrance exam was: "What is risk?" Candidates have one-hour to argue their points on risk and demonstrate they can structure an argument and follow it through to its logical conclusion, and articulate alternative views.

One student answered with just two words: "This is."

It may be an urban myth, but it's a good one. In those two words, the student captured the essence of risk from a philosophical point of view in a way that encompassed all different narratives and logical conclusions. If you really stop and think about risk and reflect on that one answer, it reveals its beautiful simplicity.

The reality of risk in our everyday lives is infinitely more complex. The greater the perceived benefit of something, the higher our tolerance for risk in that activity. For example, I want to go into space. It's been a lifelong fascination of mine: space, planets, astrophysics, gravity, time dilation, and why stuff out there is the way it is. Black holes are astonishing things. The very fact they are so dense that not even light can escape befuddles my mind every day.

As a child, I had a huge glow-in-the-dark moon poster on the ceiling above my bed. I used to hold my bedside lamp up to it at the extremity of the cord to "charge" it before bedtime. With my autistic mind I would make sure it received an equal charge all over or I'd have to start again! Between that and aviation, my fascination with space was born.

In my very early years, aged about 10 I guess, I wanted to be a fighter pilot and an astronaut. What little boy doesn't? Of course, I had absolutely no appreciation of the risk involved, just dreamy-eyed benefits: adrenalin, excitement, and the view!

My dreams came crashing down at RAF Biggin Hill when I was 15 and applied for a sixth form scholarship to be a pilot in the Royal Navy. It was the day of the aircrew aptitude test, and it's fair to say I didn't have the coordination skills to be a pilot. I was only 15.

But I did extremely well on the navigator aptitude tests: maths, verbal reasoning, spatial orientation, multitasking, and focus.

In fact, to this day, I think I am the only aviator I know who doesn't need to turn the map around to face the direction of flight. I find it easier to keep the map aligned to the north and just know that I have to turn left even though I'm travelling down the map and it looks like a right turn. My instructors struggled with this during my training as they tried to assess what I was doing. I'm just wired like that.

So, I didn't make it as a pilot, but I made it as a navigator, hence my moniker: The Financial Navigator. I graduated with my Wings from operational flying training at the top of my class. But risk was still a concept that only really hit home when friends and colleagues started to die in flying accidents.

Despite having direct exposure to the consequences of aviation risk, my fascination with space continues. I have paid a deposit for a seat on Virgin Galactic; it's going to be one hell of a ride. And not without risk. But the benefit to me, the perceived benefit, outweighs any risk. I also know I'm about 600 in the queue so it'll be roughly the 100th fee-paying flight —so others will have already taken greater risks than me.

I will, of course, cross my fingers and I will be certain to have the family financial affairs in order, just in case. Despite the risk of leaving my kids without their father, my wife without her husband, I'm going to do it come hell or high water. I can't see myself not doing it because I know how much the experience will mean to me.

And that is the essence of risk. Do the benefits outweigh the dangers? There is no right answer to that question as we all perceive benefits differently and we all assess risks differently. Ultimately, these are all subjective opinions. The role of the Financial Navigator is to help tease out these subjective views and design solutions to match.

There is no right and wrong when it comes to risk mitigation. Sure, there are generally accepted principles and I have a duty of care to my clients to make sure they are aware of and understand financial risks, but it is the client's choice whether they accept any recommendations and the risks that may come with them.

Let's dive into leg one of the three-legged stool. Starting with regret.

No Regrets

We all have regrets. One benefit of ageing is that we learn different things, our views change, and we're able to reflect on our past actions and see them in a different light. This can lead to regrets, when we wished we'd done things differently.

Take my fascination with space. I have a chance to do something I've always wanted to do, and I know if I don't go into space, I will look back from my deathbed with regret. I don't want to feel any regret when my time comes. I want to feel like I've had a full and fulfilling life, that I've left a lasting positive impression on my children, and they can feel proud of who I am and what I've done. And that means no regrets.

The problem here is we suffer with cognitive bias; the "it'll not happen to me" syndrome. Well, rest assured, death will happen to you. And taxes. The question is whether death will come when you can least afford it.

The risk of dying in space with Virgin Galactic is hard to quantify, but I can tell you with near certainty the statistical likelihood of someone from any specific age group dying. Look at the table on the next page.

We know it's going to happen at some point. Yet, we still seem to believe we're invincible. There's plenty of research to support this, too. Put simply, our brains do their best to shield us from the fear of death. Scientists believe this is a biological protection mechanism which is crucial to our ability to live in the present and accept an element of risk in everything we do.

Most of us drive cars. Some of us who drive cars fear flying. Yet we are far more likely to die in a car crash than a plane crash. The statistics vary on this, but we are roughly 100 times more likely to die in a car crash. We're also more likely to die in a plane crash than win the lottery; about 45 times more likely in any year. Still, we get in our car and drive to the Co-Op to buy a lottery ticket, before jetting off on holiday. We then have a few drinks at the airport (adding to health risks) to manage our fear of flying.

We are completely irrational about risk. This is an important point, and it's why managing the financial consequences of risk is an important part of what I do. Because left to our own devices, we bury our heads in the sand and hope the worst won't happen. We don't really believe death, critical illness, or serious injury will happen to us.

But, unfortunately, death and disaster happens all the time —as shown in this Risk Reality Table:[1]

Gender	Age Now	Risk of... (before age 67)			
		Death	Suffering a Serious Illness	Unable to work for two months or more	Any of the first three happening
Male	25	5%	16%	33%	40%
Male	30	5%	16%	32%	39%
Male	35	5%	16%	31%	38%
Male	40	6%	15%	29%	36%
Male	45	6%	15%	27%	34%
Male	50	6%	13%	24%	31%
Male	55	5%	11%	20%	26%
Male	60	4%	8%	14%	19%
Female	25	4%	14%	42%	46%
Female	30	4%	13%	40%	45%
Female	35	4%	13%	39%	44%
Female	40	4%	12%	36%	41%
Female	45	4%	11%	33%	38%
Female	50	4%	10%	29%	34%
Female	55	3%	8%	24%	28%
Female	60	3%	5%	16%	20%
Couple[11]	25	9%	28%	61%	68%
Couple	30	9%	27%	59%	67%
Couple	35	9%	27%	57%	65%
Couple	40	10%	26%	55%	63%
Couple	45	10%	24%	51%	59%
Couple	50	9%	22%	46%	55%
Couple	55	8%	19%	38%	47%
Couple	60	6%	13%	28%	35%

Risk Reality Table

What if it Happens to You?

On November 5, 2006, at 7.30 pm, as fireworks went off around the hospice, my 32-year-old brother Julian died of cancer. It's quite emotional writing this because today also happens to be his birthday.

It's an odd coincidence that I'm writing about mitigating financial risk on his birthday. If things had been different, I'd no doubt be an uncle now, and my children would know and love their uncle. Neither of these things will ever come to pass and whilst I can't do anything about it, it still fills me with regret every day.

The experience taught me to make the most of life, although it probably took me 10 years to realise it (but that's another story). It also taught me to make sure I manage the financial consequences of risk for me, my family, and my business. I want to make sure everything is neat and tidy for those I leave behind.

Then there's the 55-year-old business owner I spoke to, married with two young children, who kept saying he needed to do the things we had spoken about—but never got around to actually doing them. Despite many efforts, sorting his finances out was never important enough for him to actually book the meeting. Sadly, he only has a few months to live, and he can't insure his half of the value of his business for his wife. He's left it too late because he believed the worst would not happen to him.

Then there's the neighbour who knocked on my colleague's front door and explained that his wife had just been diagnosed with MS. Could he do anything to help with getting some insurance? I'm sorry, but it's now too late; insurers generally won't cover pre-existing conditions.

An investment in life insurance is an investment in your loved one's financial stability and your peace of mind. I can't wrap you in cotton wool and keep you physically safe, but I can help you cushion the impact of any misfortune for your family.

Don't leave it too late.

Be Prepared

Whilst we can fairly accurately predict the risk of death for people in different age groups, it's much harder to predict the chance of a financial emergency. Because shit happens and when it happens, it always happens at the worst possible time. It's Murphy's Law in action: if it can go wrong, it will go wrong.

The boiler stops working in the first cold snap, the car breaks down just when you have to be somewhere, you lose a major client, and your top performing salesperson is off sick for three months. Something will always happen that brings unexpected costs, and we need to save for it. We need to have an emergency fund to cover the rainy day.

But how much do we need? £5,000? £10,000? Well, it depends.

To understand how much you should save for an emergency, you first need to understand how much you spend.

"All of it" isn't a good answer! You'd be surprised how many people have absolutely no idea how much they spend. Or what they spend it on. Some comes in, some goes out, and that's that. But it's crucial to know your numbers, personally and in your business.

You can't turn your business from a cash-eating monster into a profit-making machine if you don't know what it's eating! Put your business on a healthy diet. Feed it well, nurture and care for it, just like you should with your own body. (Note the "should"—most of us use and abuse our bodies until it's too late; more regret!)[2]

I can guess how you're feeling at this point. I've brought up the subject of numbers again and you're already backing away. Do you look forward to the annual meeting with your accountant, where you get bamboozled with numbers that bear no relation to how much you have in your pocket or how you're feeling about your business, at the end of which you get told how much tax you must pay?

And you're left thinking, "How the hell did that happen?" For many business owners, it's a bit of a shit experience.

Of course, there are good accountants and bad

accountants, just as there are good financial advisers and bad financial advisers. If you have a bad accountant and you're blinded by numbers you don't understand—or perhaps don't even care about—find a better one. Find someone who can make the numbers simple and show you how to make sense of them so they're useful to you. If they can't present the information in a simple and meaningful way, they're not doing their job properly.

You don't have to stick with them.

It's the same in my industry. I know there are regulatory aspects that we have to cover, but most people in my industry present financial information in a way that is guaranteed to put you to sleep. It's no wonder the prospect of financial advice leads to "tomorrow thinking".

"I can't think about this now. I'll do it tomorrow," which, along with, "it'll never happen to me" is a recipe for financial ruin. Grit your teeth, get off your backside, and do something about your financial situation now. You'll not regret it.

Don't get to retirement age, realise you can't afford to retire, then wish you'd prepared properly. Find an adviser and take action. Now.

One of my clients had a complex loan arrangement with his business. In his mind, the business loaned him the profits, rather than extracting the profits and paying the tax. In reality, he was deferring an income tax liability until a later date; it would still need to be paid. One day, he would have to repay the loan to his business and extract some profit as income. All he was doing was kicking the tax can down the road. But he didn't fully appreciate this because his accountant hadn't made it clear.

Now, I'm sure the accountant provided the information— at least, he said he did—but he didn't check that my client understood (which he clearly didn't).

It got worse, though. My client was using the "loan" to offset his mortgage, to reduce the amount of interest he paid on it. The mortgage interest rate was about 1.5%, so he was borrowing £200,000 to save 1.5% in interest every year, saving approximately £3,000 in mortgage interest. This sounds good until you realise that my client was paying 2.5% interest to the business for the loan; the loan was not interest free. He was spending £5,000 a year in loan interest payments to save himself £3,000 a year of mortgage interest.

This had been going on for years and he had absolutely no idea this setup was costing him £2,000 a year. He thought he was saving money.

The accountant insisted that he'd fully informed my client about all of this. I'm sure he had, but the accountant's responsibility is to do more than inform; it is to ensure full understanding. I have the same responsibility to my clients. Understanding, not gobbledygook.

I like the original meaning behind the word client, from ancient Rome: "one who leans on another for protection." My clients are under my protection, as far as their financial wellbeing is concerned.

But the responsibility goes both ways: you need to know your numbers. If you're still giving your accountant a shoebox full of receipts at the end of the year, then you won't have much of an idea about where your money is coming from, and where it's going. The good news is this is very easily and inexpensively fixed.

The best way to get to know your numbers in the simplest terms is to use cloud accounting software. I use Xero, and there are others that are just as good. Your accountant should be able to help you understand the software and make use of the features that will help you understand your numbers. If they can't or won't help you, please find a new accountant. There are plenty of fantastic ones out there, who talk to their clients every week to discuss income and expenditure, cashflow and profit.

Your involvement in your accounting should be more than

an annual conversation about the past. That's just history and most accountants are historians, happy to review your numbers months after the event and tell you how the business performed and how much tax you need to pay. That's fine. You need to know this stuff for no other reason than to keep HMRC off your back.

Much more exciting and useful, though, is looking forwards at where your finances could be. What are your projections? Where could you save money, and where could you make more?

All that information is in your books, if you know where and how to look for it.

Frankly, I couldn't care less about my business performance nine or more months ago, other than as a comparison, because I'm dealing with the here-and-now. I dealt with my past performance nine months ago.

And that's what you need your numbers and your accountant or financial adviser to do: help you make sense of the here-and-now. How much do you spend and on what? How much is fixed cost and how much is variable cost? When do the costs hit (affecting your cashflow)? What's your profit margin? Good consultants will help you perform scenario analysis to consider the future impact of business decisions, like pricing.

For your personal finances, you can download bank statements and keep them in a spreadsheet like Excel, or you can use software packages for personal finances, too. Look at something like MoneyHub, and there are others. New pieces of software are constantly being developed; find something that suits you and learn how to use it.

The right software will help you build a picture of your finances. It will automatically categorise income and expenditure for you, which you can use to review monthly reports (simple bar graphs and charts that are easy to understand) to monitor what's going on in your business and personal finances. You must do this. If your accountant isn't doing it for you, then ask them to do it or find a new accountant.

Building the Walls: Protecting Yourself

You (or your accountant) need to do a bit of work to analyse your numbers so you can figure out how much money to keep aside for emergencies. This "emergency fund" will build a financial wall to protect your business (and family) when the cold north wind blows, to keep the dogs at bay and give you a chance to fix things and get back on track. This applies as much to your business as it does to your personal finances. I'll cover both in this section.

Your expenditure comes in two forms, which I introduced previously. Your business has fixed costs and variable costs. Fixed costs are those you pay even if you sell nothing for a month, like your office rent, staff salaries, pensions, insurance, vehicles, heat, light, software licenses. Variable costs are those that you incur only when you sell something, like buying the parts to make the stuff you sell or fuel for the van.

We're interested in fixed costs here. How much does it cost you to run the business, before you sell a widget? Remember, you need to sell enough widgets to cover the variable cost of producing and selling it, plus the fixed costs of running the business. Then you can start making a profit for you.

Your personal finances are similar: you have essential costs and discretionary costs. Essentials are things you can't turn off, like your mortgage or rent, utility bills (gas, water, electricity), life insurance, and food. This is money you still need to spend even if you stop spending on everything else. Discretionary spending is money you could save if you really had to, like holidays, clothes, and eating out.

In your business, it's a good idea to keep a multiple of your fixed costs aside as cash. In your personal life, it's a good idea to keep a multiple of your essential spending. But what is a multiple?

Everyone's individual circumstances are different, but a good rule of thumb is to put aside an absolute minimum of three months' expenditure. So, if your business costs £5,000 a month to run, then you need a minimum of £15,000 in emergency funds. But that's an absolute minimum. Ideally, you would increase this to six months, depending on your other circumstances. For some businesses with long lead times on sales, it's a good idea to keep twelve months of emergency cash.

How much you decide to put away depends on your business type, the number of clients you have, what you sell, and how much you sell. A good consultant will help you analyse and assess your business to determine what size emergency fund will be best for you. You may start by saving three months' cash, then gradually increase this pot over time.

Whatever strategy you choose, it will be individual to you and your circumstances.

The same applies to your personal finances. As a bare minimum, you need to keep three months of essential expenditure in cash. Instant access cash—not invested. Actual cash you can put your hands on at a moment's notice. That doesn't mean banknotes stuffed under the mattress; it means cash in an instant access savings account.

If you're a disciplined business owner, and it's the right thing for you to do, you can be tax efficient by keeping your emergency personal cash in the business until you need it. That way, you don't pay hefty income tax on it just to put it straight into a personal savings account. That would be pointless.

Just make sure the amount you have allocated in business cash for personal emergency reserves also covers the income tax due when you take it out. Your accountant or financial adviser can work that out for you. Make sure you take your accountant's advice on this because there are accounting implications regarding holding cash on a business sale.

If you don't have three months' worth of your business fixed costs and your personal essential costs put away, then get saving. Look long and hard at your personal discretionary spend and ask yourself if you really need to do everything this month.

Could you get a takeout and a bottle of wine instead of going to that expensive restaurant? Do you really need those new clothes? Does the business really need to sponsor the local football team (have you actually had any business from it?)

Open a bank account specifically for your emergency funds and only ever touch it in a proper emergency. Better still, open the emergency funds bank account at a different bank to your usual one and don't set up online banking. Dispose of the chequebook, too. That way, you remove the balance from sight and therefore temptation.

Oh, and running out of wine, beer, or gin doesn't count as an emergency!

There are caveats to all this, though. If you have bad debt, like high-interest credit cards, then save one month of your essential costs or fixed costs, then start paying down that expensive debt as quickly as you can. If you have an emergency, you can use the credit card again; but if you don't have an emergency, you'll save yourself a stack of credit card interest. Once you've paid off the debt, throw away the credit card and finish saving for that emergency fund.

Credit cards are bad debt: stay well away from them if you can.

With an emergency stash of cash comes a certain level of comfort and relief. You'll worry less. You'll sleep better at night. You'll know you can weather a strong north wind because you've built sturdy walls of emergency cash around you.

Start by putting away three months of costs, but always

look at your specific circumstances. It might be better for you to put away six, nine, or even twelve months' funds. That's why it's important to seek professional advice. If the adviser tries to sell you insurance without understanding your circumstances, walk away and find someone who will look closely at your circumstances and develop a meaningful financial plan with you.

If you do the work and figure out your business's fixed costs, and your personal essential expenditure, *and* you have three months' worth of cash put away as an emergency fund: congratulations! No, really—you are leagues ahead of most people. Give yourself a pat on the back and have a night out. You deserve it. Well done.

Keeping out the Rain

Once you've built your walls, your next step is protection. Protection is the industry term for insurance; protecting your financial wellbeing.

Death is certain (hopefully a long time from now), but it is actually the least likely insurable event to occur before age 67. Statistically, it's much more likely that you'll be diagnosed with a life-threatening illness or be unable to work for two months or more before age 67. We typically use age 67 as by 2028, 67 will be the state retirement age, and it's the age when most people aim to retire.[3]

Now, if you have a mortgage and young children, if your partner isn't working, and it's going to take you a year to save your emergency fund, then there might be a balance to strike between life insurance now and saving for emergencies.

There's no right answer here, but you might want to take out life insurance to cover the mortgage payments (which is pretty cheap, by the way) alongside saving for emergencies. It might mean it takes a little longer to fill the emergency fund, but that's okay. Once the emergency fund is full, you can top up your insurance and/or start making investments for your future wealth. Sometimes, making investments alongside saving for the emergency fund is an appropriate strategy. It all depends on your circumstances, which is why it's impossible to share the "best" overall strategy that'll make sure you're fine.

It really isn't as simple as that. Beware of anyone who tells you it is.

There is much more to life insurance than simply heading to one of the comparison websites and pressing the buy button. Please don't do it that way. You'll probably end up with something that isn't suitable and doesn't protect you in the way you would like.

Instead, work with a financial expert to get the right policy for you, your family, and your business. There's a popular myth that says online life insurance is vastly cheaper than going through an adviser. It isn't.

It's also much more complicated than simply buying £100,000 of life insurance and thinking you're covered. Trust me, I'm the Financial Navigator.

A good advisor will help you think about your business and personal risks, find out what you already have in place to meet those risks, identify options to close the gaps, and develop a financial plan to mitigate your risks.

For example, you might have other resources you could rely on, like a second home, or wealthy parents to help you out if things get tough. That is a perfectly valid risk management strategy, as long as it works for you, and you have actually agreed it with your parents.

This is the value of getting sound advice: it means you actually work out a plan, make sure the plan is viable, agree it, and document it. And then you actually do it. An airy-fairy idea isn't a plan, it's just that: an idea.

I won't get into the technicalities of insurance here, other than to say that there's a lot to consider and it can be complicated—because humans are complicated. You might

worry that taking out life insurance is going to be expensive—
and you may be right. It's easy to over-insure yourself and
end up spending a fortune if you don't know what you're
doing.

But life insurance is a solid investment.

Don't think about insurance as wasted money. It isn't. It's
as much an investment in your family and business wellbeing
as saving money is. Why? Because when you buy life
insurance, you're buying peace of mind—and peace of mind
is invaluable for the ones left behind (not to mention one less
thing for you to worry about while you're still here).

Let's carry out a quick self-assessment using the questions
below. If your answer to every question is acceptable, you're
either fibbing, extremely wealthy, or the only person I've met
who has actually thought about this and actioned it. In which
case you can probably put this book down and do something
else!

Imagine this: you died yesterday. Unexpectedly. It's the
morning after, and you're sitting on a cloud looking down at
your loved ones. What financial carnage have you left behind?

- Who will pay the mortgage, buy food, and pay for
  holidays?
- Can your family afford to live in your home
  without having to work at a time of significant
  emotional stress? For how long?
- Who will run the business? Who will close the
  business? Who will sell the business? Is it fit to sell?
- Would you be happy if your deceased business
  partner's wife/husband/partner took part in the
  business or, rightly, demanded their 50% of the
  profits that only you are now working for?
- Does your family know what insurance policies you
  have and with whom? Are they in Trust? Should
  they be in Trust?[4]

- Who will deal with the insurance company to make the claim?
- What funeral arrangements do you want?
- Have you made provision in your Will for your family to receive your assets as you would wish?
- What happens to the value of your home if your widowed partner remarries?

Give Them a Chance to Grieve and Breathe

Broadly speaking, you should first insure any debt you have, so your death wipes the debt slate clean. This gives your loved ones a chance to grieve and breathe. This means it pays the mortgage off, which is probably your biggest cost. It gives your family breathing room, safe in the knowledge they will keep a roof over their heads. How would your family feel having just lost you and knowing they have no means to pay the mortgage? Unless you have underlying medical conditions, it's also pretty cheap, so it's a no-brainer, really.

Things get a little tougher after that. You have a menu of choices, trading off risk mitigation against cost. I've mentioned before that you can easily over-insure yourself and spend way more than you need. But as risk is a subjective thing and personal to you, your experiences, and your perception of the future, there is no real right and wrong. Think through your needs and options carefully, get quotes, and analyse them to find the optimum solution that gives you enough peace of mind without breaking the bank.

Your choices centre around easing the financial consequences of illness or injury, and providing for your family after death. Even with the mortgage paid off, can your family afford to live without your income? Probably not, if you're the main breadwinner and have young children. So, we can close the gap by providing an income to your partner for a period, usually until the children have left school, but it could be longer. Or you could provide an extra lump sum that can be invested to support your family for a few years. There are plenty of options here. Again, because it is life insurance, it's relatively cheap.

What happens if you have a heart attack, cancer, stroke, or similar? Will you be able to work? What's your sick pay entitlement, if any? Would you have to go back to work sooner than you should because you need the income? If the first heart attack doesn't kill you, the second one surely will.

You can buy insurance that pays a lump sum if you are diagnosed with a range of specified critical illnesses. Contrary to popular opinion, if you are open and honest with your medical history and you are diagnosed with an insured illness, the plan will pay out. You can use this money however you like, but most people use it to pay off the mortgage, or at least some of the mortgage, and provide some additional funds to change the home if you need to manage your illness. Most people don't think about the potential need to move house or change their home to accommodate the consequences of sickness or injury. You might need to adapt your home to help you live a normal life.

What happens if you're involved in a car accident and can't work for six or nine months? What if you get sick and can't work? How will you pay the bills?

You can insure for this, too, and if you're self-employed and the sole income earner, I'd suggest you give this one some serious thought.

Scaffolder? Broken your leg? That's no income for at least six weeks.

But you can take out an insurance plan that pays replacement income for the period you cannot work. If you get back to work but get sick again and have to have more time off, the plan will replace your income again.

There are restrictions on income levels and many other options and considerations, but you get the point: it's relatively easy and inexpensive to protect yourself and your family should the worst happen.

"I hear you, Nick, but I'm still invincible and I still don't think it will happen to me."

Let's hope so. But just in case, let's do it, anyway. I guarantee that if anything were to happen to you, your surviving family will be grateful you protected their financial security.

Remember, bad things happen to good people, like my brother Julian. We have no control over it. But we can make sure your affairs are in order for those you leave behind.

What's Next?

It's time to get to know your numbers if you're serious about finding, growing, and keeping the wealth in your business (and family). Start by booking an appointment with your accountant to figure out where you are, and where you want to go—and what tools will help you get there.

Then take these simple steps:

1. Set up a bank account for your business emergency fund and one for your personal emergency fund. Start paying into it straight away. Aim for three months' expenses to start with.
2. Go through the questions on page 143, then use it to make a plan for you and your family, should the worst happen.
3. Talk to an expert about protecting your loved ones financially. At the very least, make sure you cover your mortgage payments.

13

TAXATION AND BITTER PILLS
A DIFFERENT WAY OF LOOKING AT TAX BILLS

When I crossed the line, I paid my respects to King Neptune with a shave, a bitter pill, and a wash to atone for my crimes. We were in the middle of the Indian Ocean, an awfully long way from land, and we were crossing the equator. I, and many others of the Ship's Company of HMS York, were presented to Neptune's Court for the infamous Crossing the Line Ceremony.

Naval tradition dictates that any ship crossing the equator must pay their respects to the Lord of the Seas, King Neptune, to gain his acceptance. I was charged for my "crimes" and justice was meted out.

I have to say, the Naval chefs really know how to make a bitter pill out of flour, water, and heaven knows what else. It was truly revolting.

As with so many sayings, "crossing the line" has its origins in the nautical world. It means going too far; pushing your luck. In the Navy, we appease Neptune, god of the sea, with a bitter pill.

If you cross the line with HMRC, though, you'll get far more than a bitter pill to swallow.

Tax: Beverley's favourite topic! It's guaranteed to put her

to sleep in seconds. It's amazing how different we are, and yet so similar too. I love finding ways to save tax; her eyes glaze over at the mere mention of the word. My wife has absolutely no interest in tax, doesn't understand it, and doesn't *want* to understand it. Her attitude towards money is quite different to mine. I'm organised and efficient; she hasn't a clue how much money we have, or don't have, or where it's saved and invested.

I remember when we first met: she had one high street bank account, one building society savings account, and one cash ISA. She had quite a few thousand in her bank account earning almost no interest. It was simple and worked for her, but it appalled me; that money should work for her, not reduce in value because of inflation!

Beverley told me a story about running down the high street at 2.55 pm on April 5, clutching a bag full of cash she'd just withdrawn from her building society to get it to her bank to pay into her ISA before 3 pm.

She's a last-minute kind of person. I'm a planner. It's a funny combination, but it works for us. We spend a lot of time laughing with each other and at each other's foibles.

Crossing the Line

For me, tax efficiency means operating within the rules whereas tax evasion is a crime that steals money out of the pockets of those who abide by the law. Tax evasion crosses the line. Tax evasion is theft from all of us, but many don't seem to see things that way.

Some people think being tax efficient is immoral. Some think it is their responsibility to avoid paying tax entirely, through illegal means (a little white collar crime). For some, tax evasion is a sport and an occupational hazard.

It's an interesting study in morality, taxes. After all, we're preventing the government getting its greedy hands on our hard-earned cash, right?

Wrong.

It's been my experience that small-time, often accidental landlords seem to think it's okay to evade paying tax on their rental income. They deliberately choose not to declare that rental income to HMRC. This is fascinating because these are otherwise law-abiding citizens in every way, and yet they think not paying tax on their rental income isn't really a crime. It is. There is, in some people, a self-righteous view that they shouldn't pay tax on their property income and anyway, HMRC will never know.

If you are one of those people, I have bad news for you: HMRC is getting really good at finding you. The world of big data and AI is making it easier to spot data anomalies. For example, the Land Registry holds the deeds for most properties in the UK, which list the owner's names. Your tenant pays council tax (or claims a student exemption or perhaps some sort of benefit). If the name of the person paying council tax at the property doesn't match the name of the owner at the Land Registry, but the property owner's tax return doesn't include any information on rental income, HMRC will dig in and start looking around. It's not that difficult.

People don't generally like deliberate tax evaders and they'll happily report it to HMRC. I heard a second-hand story about a chap at one of the golf clubs I attend. Apparently, he'd been telling people how he didn't pay any tax on his rental income. He got caught soon after his bragging session and had to pay his tax plus penalties.

The penalties for this sort of tax evasion, where you don't voluntarily come clean, can be up to 100% of the unpaid tax. Which means you pay the tax due plus the same again. Double your original tax bill. If you voluntarily come clean, the penalties will be lower and may even be reduced to zero; it depends if the unpaid tax was deliberate or an error.

HMRC has a Let Property Campaign which is open-ended: people can self-declare their unpaid rental income before they're caught—which is a much better way to do it. The aftermath of COVID-19 is inevitably going to lead to tax increases, and more pressure to minimise tax leakage through undeclared and underpaid tax. The Making Tax Digital scheme will help HMRC identify tax evaders, and you can expect HMRC to pursue you vigorously if you're one of them.

There will probably be a public campaign to urge people to identify those evading tax. We will all have to pay for COVID, eventually. It doesn't seem fair that honest business owners should bear the brunt of it.

Then there are the deliberate tax evaders who are happy to pay "different" taxes. The middle-England couple with a small property portfolio, maybe three or four rental houses. What they haven't told you is they pay no tax on their rental income. It all started when they first met, moved in together, and kept one property. At the time, the mortgage exceeded the income, so they were making a loss. As time went by this changed, and rather than manage the loss to profit transition, they simply elected to carry on not declaring anything. They now have several properties, all without mortgages, making decent "tax-free" undeclared income.

They don't see their actions as criminal and they don't believe they'll get caught, so they carry on evading tax that is legally due. They are taking money from the pockets of others. It is theft, pure and simple.

But they also have a potential inheritance tax problem for the kids and a capital gains tax problem. Capital gains tax is due on any increase in the property value when (if) they sell a rented property.[1] They obviously don't want to pay more tax than they have to—that's clear from their illegal tax-evasion activities—yet they seem happy for their kids to eventually pay 40% inheritance tax on their properties.

The thing is, with proper planning they could volunteer the unpaid income tax, regulate their circumstances, and manage inheritance tax and capital gains tax effectively, paying much less tax than they might think. Plus, they'll be able to sleep easy in their beds.

The Moral Compass

Our stance on tax is a choice. I will not work with clients who believe that tax evasion is their duty or their right, particularly when it comes to property income. It is our collective duty and to our collective benefit to operate within the law set by Parliament.

I am not a fan of tax evaders, but tax efficiency is perfectly legitimate, and I have absolutely no issue with improving a client's tax position within the rules. I have a big issue with those who deliberately avoid tax, though. It is theft. They are stealing from our pockets because our tax money part-funds our public services: the NHS, education, armed services, local government. The more tax they avoid, the more tax the rest of us have to pay—which means they're taking money out of our pockets to line their pockets. It's criminal, and it's wrong. If we wish to live in our society and benefit from the services we all receive, then we all need to contribute our fair share.

It's up to Parliament and the Government to determine what "fair" is. Naturally, that question will always lead to some debate!

Taxation is a polarising topic. Some hate it, believing taxation is theft, and pay as little as possible. Others believe it is our moral duty to pay our taxes in full and not seek to be efficient with our tax planning.

I believe strongly that the Government sets the rules and as long as you operate within the rules, that's perfectly okay.

Whether a particular aspect of tax efficiency is within the spirit of the rules is one for Parliament or the courts to make, not me and certainly not HMRC. HMRC has a habit of aggressively stating its tax position in a way that effectively threatens the recipient of a tax investigation. They sometimes go beyond reasonable behaviour. It is not for HMRC to decide guilt or innocence, that is for the courts. The problem is, the rules aren't always as black and white as they might seem.

In 2018, Polly Toynbee, *The Guardian* columnist, wrote an article about a tax planning seminar she attended. She was scathing about the ways in which perfectly legal tax planning is carried out. Her point was that someone has to pay for the NHS, the armed forces, and other such bastions of our society. To quote the article, "Tax relief has become a gigantic welfare state for the well-off."

I understand her point, but we (my industry) don't make the rules, we simply apply the rules for the benefit of our clients—and we have a professional obligation to do so. Pointedly seeking to shame and demonise finance professionals for abiding by the law is unhelpful and only serves to place a further barrier between those in need of advice and those providing it.

I understand Polly is trying to raise awareness amongst her readership which may galvanise action to create change, and that's perfectly fine. In fact, setting aside the way she implies immoral behaviour on our part, and looking purely at the sentiment of the story, she is right. Our tax system desperately needs an overhaul. There is clearly a balance to strike between a disproportionate tax burden on the wealthy and our collective responsibility as human beings to help those less fortunate than ourselves.

Our current system is archaic, way too complicated, and changes far too frequently, which makes it hard for people to plan for their future. Our tax system is ultimately a political tool and is therefore subject to the vagaries of election timing to win votes. That will always mean there is a political imperative influencing taxation decisions. Making tax changes might be a good lever for votes, but is it really the right thing to do?

All that aside, I have a professional obligation to give my clients advice that is right for them. This includes ensuring that taxation does not erode the value of their wealth and using tax-efficient mechanisms to help a client achieve their goals. We often work with accountants to do this by planning for the future and considering taxation as part of the wealth management mix.

Consider this example. A client comes to me wanting to invest £20,000. I recommend they open a general investment account and invest in various funds. This type of investment is subject to taxation on gains and income. It could tip my client into a different tax bracket, which could impact their pension contributions and their long-term wealth prospects. It could compound a capital gains tax problem for them. Alternatively, I could recommend an ISA where gains and income are tax free. Considering Polly's argument, is it right that I recommend a tax-efficient government-designed savings account to protect my client's investment from taxation?

Of course it is. I have a professional obligation to do so.

Taking Polly's argument to its natural conclusion, I should not recommend the ISA because there will always be someone less well-off who doesn't have £20,000 to invest in an ISA, and so this "rich" person should volunteer to pay more tax by investing outside an ISA. Polly is deciding where she believes the line to be, although she isn't clear at what amount of wealth one should stop being tax efficient at.

Tax planning through the use of Trusts and other such schemes is perfectly legitimate, but typically the preserve of those with sufficient wealth to protect. The ultimate effect is that the wealthy can, in specific circumstances, end up paying less tax as a proportion of their overall income or wealth. The less wealthy rarely benefit from these tax planning options as they don't have enough wealth to protect, or their wealth will not be taxed through inheritance, anyway.

The pound and pence amount of tax paid by the wealthy remains a significant number, it's just a lower proportion of their overall wealth through careful tax planning.

What gets missed in this debate is the risk that comes with some tax planning opportunities—and the fact the Government designed them, not the financial services industry. I take issue with Polly's article as she states tax efficiency is "tax avoiding via trusts, gift plans, loan schemes, equity release, the enterprise investment scheme…" none of which are tax evasion. They are legitimate tax-planning options available to everyone.

They may be tax efficient, but they are not tax evasion. The former is legal, the latter is not.

Take the Enterprise Investment Scheme, for example. The Government introduced it to incentivise investment into smaller unlisted UK companies. The scheme comes with tax reliefs, established by the Government. The industry didn't invent it to help the rich avoid taxation; the Government created the scheme to reward those making high-risk investments to help power the economy.

The difficulty with making these moral judgements is exactly that: it's a judgement. I don't see it as my role to judge the rights or wrongs of legislation. My role is to make sure I fully understand the legislation and the tax planning opportunities open to my clients. It is my responsibility and my duty of care to explain to clients how they can minimise their tax burden.

Not everyone will accept my recommendations, and that's perfectly fine. But it's not for me to judge.

Ultimately, the Government sets the rules and if the Government doesn't like the way we use the rules, then it should change the rules.

Fifty Shades of Grey

Taxation is a grey area, and HMRC isn't the most helpful sometimes. Take the example of the business owner with a fair bit of cash in their business. They've taken plenty of risk to get where they are. They employ people; they power the economy; and they bear the risk—why shouldn't they reap the reward? They know they need a pension, so they're advised to put £120,000 into their pension directly from the business using pension carry-forward rules. This is one of the most tax efficient ways to extract profit from the business.

The Government sets the rules, not me.

Because there is an element of business tax planning involved and I'm not an accountant, the accountant needs to confirm the pension contribution is allowable as a business expense to reduce corporation tax. If it's not an allowable expense, then there is no corporation tax saving, and it becomes an inefficient way to get the money into a pension.

All accountants accept this is perfectly legitimate tax planning, defined in the rules to allow businesses to make owner pension contributions backdated by three years (there are other specific criteria to meet, so speak to an expert first).

The purpose is to account for the fact that businesses sometimes need to make expensive investment decisions, which can mean the owners, who are taking the risk, don't have sufficient profit to make pension contributions in some years. It's a way to even the playing field and allow businesses to manage cash flow, investment, and profit extraction over a longer time frame.

But, strictly speaking, no accountant can actually confirm a pension contribution is an allowable business expense. And you can't ask HMRC before doing it. The only way to know for sure is to do it, submit the corporation tax return, then ask HMRC. It's a ridiculous system. Most accountants understand this and know it's perfectly normal, but some may not and don't understand the rules.

We often have to interpret very complex rules and make a professional judgement about what's acceptable. That is what you pay a professional for: their professional expertise.

Legislation provides tax-efficient mechanisms, and we use those to save money for our clients. It's no different to managing investments to *make* money for our clients. The net effect is the same: increased net wealth.

My usual response to someone who says this is immoral is to ask how much extra income tax they volunteer to pay? They usually reply with, "That's not the point." Actually, it is. If you're not managing taxation, you are volunteering to pay tax you don't need to pay. Simples.

It's Complicated

Throughout your life, you'll be subject to different taxes, many of which you'll be familiar with: income tax, National Insurance (yes, this is a tax!), capital gains tax, inheritance tax, stamp duty, VAT, corporation tax...

And then there's all the different reliefs and allowances, most of which you've never heard of. Most accountants and financial advisers know about these rates and reliefs, but few will apply them effectively. Why? Because most advisers are reactive and one-dimensional. Successful tax planning is multidimensional, requiring a full understanding of the rules, rigorous application, and detailed modelling of the future. The adviser who spends time modelling the future to inform decisions in the present is serving their clients well.

You'll notice that I haven't given you any specific tax planning efficiencies in this chapter. There's a good reason for that: what works for one person will not necessarily be right for another. Plus, the rules and thresholds change constantly, so any specific advice I gave would likely be out of date by the time you read it.

The biggest lesson here is to take expert advice and make sure your selected adviser is looking to the future to help you make the right decisions now.

From a moral point of view, tax planning and tax efficiency will always be hotly debated. When you look at the likes of Google, Amazon, and Facebook, all of whom have been challenged over their tax-planning practices, can you really blame them? They've not actually done anything illegal, as far as I'm aware. They have acted in accordance with their legal responsibility to maximise shareholder value, part of which is to manage taxation. If governments, and the public, don't like what they're doing, they should legislate to prevent it rather than bleat about how unfair it is. And maybe stop shopping with big corporations whose activities they object to.

It comes down to where you draw the line. For me, the line is the law. If it's within the law, then we're being tax efficient and that's okay. If it's outside the law, well, that's tax evasion and it's illegal. It's theft from your neighbours, your friends, and your family.

You will one day be caught and judged. Personally, I'd rather swallow King Neptune's bitter pill than one from HMRC.

What's Next?

Tax efficiency means managing your circumstances within the rules to minimise taxation, legally.

Tax evasion, on the other hand, is a crime. It is theft.

Instead of seeing tax as a burden, consider it a symbol of your success. The more tax you pay whilst being tax efficient, the more profit you're making in your business.

Some people still end up with unexpected tax bills. As I said earlier, that's on you and is easily avoided.

1. Work out how much tax you paid last year and divide that by how much you invoiced, e.g. £30k tax bill divided by £100k turnover = 30%.
2. Every time you get paid, save that percentage in a separate bank account every month.
3. At the end of the year, you should have enough savings to cover your tax bill, all things being equal.

14

WEALTH EXCITEMENT

"HOW MUCH HAVE MY INVESTMENTS MADE, NICK?"

I love nothing more than sitting down with one of my lovely clients and showing them growth in their investments. It's exciting. The kind of reward that activates the pleasure parts of our brains. I get a big high five and my client gets feelings of pleasure, value, and worth. I love that part of what I do. It brings me joy to make a positive difference to someone's life. It's my why.

It's not always like that, of course, because the reality is markets are driven by sentiment and collective confidence, and we human beings are far from rational. I remind all my clients: "One day, we'll sit down together, and your investments will have gone down. It's inevitable. Are you okay with that?" We then have a discussion about what that means, and how they would feel about differing levels of "down."

Five percent? Ten, twenty, thirty percent? Where do you start to feel pain? When do you get uncomfortable? It's a very personal question and very different for everybody, but I need my clients to understand that I'm not a magician. I can't control the markets. I can only show you the path and guide you along it. The path is always going to be a balancing act between competing priorities, desires, affordability, and risk. I know some risk-averse clients who elected to hold bundles of cash in the bank, unaware that the Government protection scheme safeguarded only a proportion of their cash balance.

"But Nick, £1 is still worth £1 next year. Cash is king and I know how much I've got when it's in cash. It ain't going nowhere."

I've heard that and similar arguments before, many a time. But it isn't true. £1 isn't necessarily worth £1 next year. Or to be clear, £1 can still buy you £1-worth of stuff; it's just less stuff. You get less for your money.

The Time Cost of Money

Inflation reduces the value of your money. It means your cash buys you less stuff as time goes by. I appreciate this may be a difficult concept to understand so let me explain using a Mars Bar. Imagine a Mars Bar costs £1 and all you eat is Mars Bars. Battered ones if you're from Glasgow but for argument's sake we'll say they're still £1 each.

You've put all your hard-earned £££ into various banks across the UK to stay within your Government protection limits for cash deposits. You decide to retire, and you know you have enough pounds to feed you for 20 years. Three Mars Bars a day for 365 days a year, for 20 years, equals £21,900 in bank cash deposits allocated specifically to feed you.

Perfect, you think.

Well, no, it isn't perfect because with average long-term inflation of 2%, and an assumed deposit interest rate of effectively 0%, you'll run out of money for Mars Bars in 17 years, because your Mars Bars are getting more expensive. This means you'll be hungry for the last three years.

How does that work?

Inflation is the measure of how quickly prices are increasing. There are different measures of inflation, but we'll stick to the basic principle.

If prices are increasing by 2% every year, on average, this means your Mars Bar will cost £1.02 next year. Then £1.04. Then £1.06. Then £1.08. Then £1.10. Then £1.13. In year 17 they'll cost £1.37 each.

Oops—you've run out of money to feed yourself in retirement.

This is because your £21,900 saved for 20 years to buy three Mars Bars a day has not risen in value. You are not earning interest at the same rate as inflation is increasing prices.

When we look at investing a client's cash or earnings, we need to consider inflation and the buying power of your money. If you want to buy the same number of Mars Bars every year, your money needs to grow by the same amount as prices increase (2% in this example). If you put your £1 coins in a safe deposit box they are guaranteed to grow at 0%, not accounting for the cost of the box. Inflation has reduced the value of your money, value being the measure of how much stuff you can buy with your £1.

For some people, this will not be a problem. They will have enough cash to last them until they're 150 years old, in which case the safe deposit box option might appeal! The rest of us normally need to achieve growth of at least inflation (2% in this case) so we can still buy the same amount of stuff.

Whatever you do with your cash, it comes at a cost. Depositing it with various banks to stay within government protection limits comes at a cost because the interest rate will be less than inflation. Putting physical £1 coins into safety deposit boxes across the UK and paying to insure them comes at a cost, not just for the boxes and insurance, but because your money will be worth less as inflation increases. In other words, you will always pay for someone or something to hold your cash.

But what can you do about it? Well, if you want the buying power of your money to be at least the same next year and the year after, you need to achieve a net return after taxation of at least the rate of inflation. So if inflation this year is 2% on average, then your cash needs to grow by 2% *after* any taxation on its growth, for your cash to still buy the same amount of stuff. One Mars Bar this year equals one Mars Bar next year.

This applies equally to your business and your personal finances. A chap I know runs a very successful business. His emergency cash needs for the business are about £250,000. However, he currently keeps about £750,000 in cash because it's "safe". Until I pointed out the Government will only protect a tiny proportion of that £750k. If the bank were to go under, which it nearly did in 2008, he would lose most of it.

He's earning £375 a year interest on his £750,000. That is profit in the business, so it's taxed—and he loses some of that £375 to corporation tax. It gets worse, though.

To extract that interest profit from the business, in his case, he pays higher-rate dividend tax. This means the after-tax interest on his £750,000 is £200 a year in his personal pocket.

So, he's earning £200 per year net interest. He wasn't that bothered, pointing out that he was still making something. Well, no—because inflation was running at about 2%. That £750,000 needs to grow by £15,000 every year if he wants his money to buy the same amount of stuff.

He was effectively setting fire to £14,800 a year by not at least matching inflation. That got his attention.

Now, clearly he needs some emergency cash, but he is still setting fire to nearly £10,000 a year. That's the cost of holding £500,000 in cash that could do something else. He is paying the bank £10,000 a year to store his cash.

I've simplified this scenario to make the point about inflation because it is a crucial factor when it comes to investment decision-making. It's certainly not the only factor, but it is important.

Like all things in life, investment is about balance.

So, we know we need to have emergency funds available as liquid cash and we talked about how much that should or could be in chapter 12. We know inflation erodes the value of cash, so you don't want to hold more than you need to. Which means, hopefully, we have additional cash and/or earnings to invest for our long-term future.

And that's the key to this: long-term thinking.

The problem is, long-term thinking is quite tricky for human beings. Most of us are wired to react to the here and now, and struggle to visualise the future, which isn't helpful for long-term investing. Which is why you need an expert guide to keep you on the rails.

Taking Investment Risk

To manage inflation risk, you need to take investment risk. This means investing in the "markets". That scary place where prices seem to go up and down at random. It sort of feels like putting money in, closing your eyes, and hoping for the best.

I understand that feeling. I've felt it myself. But with risk comes reward, which is borne out when you look at long-term historic investment performance.[1]

I don't advocate investing for less than three to five years. There's a good reason for this: the shorter the investment period, the greater the chance the investment will be worth less than when you started. We also need to account for fees and charges, because no investment is free.

Even if you invested in a FTSE 100 tracker on September 1, 2008, 28 days before the crash, five years later your investment would have risen by roughly 46% (excluding fees). Granted, the first six months of the investment will have been a considerable rollercoaster with a drop of roughly 35%— which is why I always talk to my clients about investment pain: the natural consequences of risk and how much you can tolerate before you crumble and walk away.

Risk is therefore a really important question and a really important part of understanding what's right for you. Yet most advisers don't spend the time to explain how risk fits into the overall plan, how investment risk is both a good and a bad thing.

Some of that is driven by the regulatory environment we live in, which is static. For example, the FCA requires advisers to assess a client's attitude to risk and thus invest their money at that level of risk. You kind of get what you're given. But very few advisers spend the time to show a client how risk is dynamic, how risk could produce different long-term outcomes, and what that might mean for them.

Let's take the example of a 40-year-old couple. Married, with two pre-teen kids. The regulated process says, broadly, that we must gather the facts, determine a client's goals, understand their attitude to risk and how much loss they could withstand, then invest their money for that goal taking into account the client's attitude to risk. The goal becomes almost secondary to risk in that risk is driving the investment decision.

If the client's goal is to retire at 55 but they haven't saved enough, and their attitude to risk is moderate, they're probably not going to reach their goal. There are three possible changes they can make to get a different outcome:

1. Invest more money, which may not be feasible.
2. Retire later, which isn't the goal.
3. Invest at higher risk.

Yet the static regulated process says risk is broadly fixed. In other words, if I were to advise a client to invest at higher risk so they have a better chance of meeting their goal, I'm on a sticky wicket. If the risk materialises and they lose money or don't make enough money, there's a potential complaint in the pipeline for investing outside the client's risk appetite.

Sometimes, it is helpful to ask, "How much risk do you *need* to take to achieve your goal?" I can then use software tools that use stochastic modelling[2] to determine the probability of an investment outcome given a particular level of risk.

This leads to a mature conversation with the client, one we can document with evidence, that says, "This is how much risk you need to take to have x% chance of achieving your objective. This is what that might mean for you in terms of potential losses during the investment time frame."

This is all statistics based on long-term historic trends, so it is never an accurate predictor of the future. It can only ever tell you what would have happened in the past, if all variables stayed the same.

These models aid understanding and help a client reach the right decision for them with as much relevant information as possible. The ultimate outcome of that discussion can be pretty much anything and is very individual.

It works the other way around too.

Why take more risk than you need? This is normally down to greed. If your objective is to retire at a particular age with a particular income, and to achieve that only requires you to invest at low-to-moderate risk, why would you invest at high risk and potentially lose more money than you might later be able to afford?

I had this conversation with someone a few years ago. He had a decent understanding of risk, statistics, modelling, and outcomes. He also had a high natural risk appetite and a history of long-term investment thinking. He was happy to leave money invested for the long-term and accept that his investment goes up and down. To achieve his aim, he didn't need to take much investment risk at all. But he wanted more. He wanted to invest at his natural risk appetite, despite not needing to.

I explained it like this.

Imagine you live in London, and you need to get to a meeting in Edinburgh. It's an eight-hour drive. The meeting is at 4 pm so you leave at 6.30 am, giving you time for a break and a cushion in case of unforeseen circumstances. The traffic gods are smiling on you, so you drive at a steady 70 mph and arrive on time, ready for the meeting, refreshed, relaxed, and raring to go. You listened to Classic FM (other radio stations are available!) which kept you calm throughout the journey. Perfect.

Or, you can do the following. You can leave at 8 am, drive at 95 mph, weave in and out of traffic, tailgate, and undertake. Maybe the traffic gods are on your side and you arrive at 3 pm, pumped up and over-excited. It's raining (well, it is Scotland) so you now spend an hour sitting in a café waiting for the meeting to start. Three days later, you get the speeding ticket that tips you into a six-month driving ban.

In the second scenario, you've deliberately taken more risk than you needed to. You've achieved your objective early for no benefit, and you now have a driving ban. You might have had a car accident of course; in which case you will have missed the meeting and missed your objective. All for the sake of risk you didn't need to take.

Risk is an integral, important and welcome part of financial planning. If there were no risk, there would be no reward. At the extreme end of taking no risk, this could manifest itself as taking your hard-earned income, converting it into £1 coins and depositing it in safety deposit boxes. The coins are real; they are securely deposited; and they are insured for theft or fire for example. Brilliant plan, except for inflation.

At the other end, you could go all-in on bitcoin. But don't: you may as well go to Vegas and play roulette.

Don't Put All Your Eggs in One Basket

Still nervous about investing? I get it; it can be complicated. Maybe investing isn't for you, which is fine! I don't mind what you do and I'm certainly not judging. But if you do invest, there is another element to risk: diversification. It's important not to put all your eggs in one basket.

Unsurprisingly, 80% of people are medium risk when it comes to investing. Having a natural risk appetite of medium doesn't mean you only put your money in medium-risk funds or shares. It means your overall investment portfolio, when considered as a whole, is medium risk. It will contain cash (low risk) and it may well contain some high-risk investments too. But overall, the risk to your investment will be medium.

Cash is a necessary part of an investment portfolio as it means you can take advantage of opportunities and pay any fees without disinvestment. This may also be important to manage taxation on your portfolio.

By investing widely, you minimise the risk of one bad investment having a disproportionate effect on the whole lot.

One way of doing this is holding investments in different geographic locations, spreading your investments across the globe. This has the effect of managing geographic risk but introduces currency risk whereby changes to the exchange rate could have a detrimental (or positive) impact on the value of your investments in your currency.

Then there's product risk to consider. If you put your total investment into one financial product, like a pension, changes to Government policy or law may disproportionately expose you to political and legislative risks. Let's say your plan to repay your mortgage was to take your 25% tax-free cash allowance from your pension at age 55 to pay it off. What happens if the government changes that rule? Would you even know the rule had changed? How would it affect you?

What about what you invest in? Think about all the different industries and sectors: agriculture and petrochemicals, engineering and biotech, pharmaceuticals and green energy. By investing across multiple sectors, you minimise the chance of issues in one sector adversely affecting your overall portfolio.

Imagine what would have happened to your investment if you held most of your money in commercial property funds when COVID-19 hit. Most of those funds closed because it was impossible to provide a meaningful valuation. This meant that because the assets in the fund—shops, offices, leisure centres, etc.—could not be realistically valued, it was impossible to value the fund itself. So the funds were closed. Nobody could get money out and nobody could put money in.

There is a long list of different risks when it comes to investments, some of which I've mentioned above. Your adviser should understand these risks, help you understand them, and consider them when making investment recommendations for you. You should design your portfolio of investments to manage these risks as much as possible. Your adviser should be able to explain the rationale for their investment recommendations and they should have a clear process in place to monitor and manage those investment recommendations to ensure they remain appropriate for you.

Creating investment portfolios based on individuals' circumstances and risk-profiles isn't easy and it is time-consuming. It requires specialist skills, and knowledge of the investment markets. I need to consider every client as an individual and think about what changes I need to make to existing investments, if any. The FCA requires advisers providing an ongoing service to review the suitability of the existing investment mix at least once a year. If that isn't happening, then you're paying for a service you're not receiving.

Yet we continue to see in my industry (and many others) a race to the bottom on price. There is a perception that being "cheap" is a good thing, when we should focus on value and service excellence (quality). Low price with high quality and high value are mutually exclusive: if an adviser is charging rock-bottom prices, they're very unlikely to be providing high-quality advice or spending the time to identify high-value investments. Which means they won't be putting the time and effort into your portfolio that you're looking for.

Price is simply a function of quality and value: the lower the price, the lower the quality and/or value. When a client asks for or expects a lower price, ask this question: "Yes, of course, no problem at all. How much quality and value shall we remove so I can lower my price?"

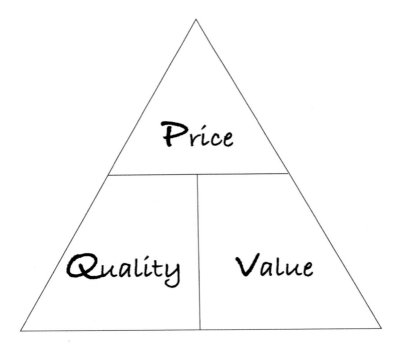

The Nirvana Triangle

I'm not suggesting you pay excessive fees for anything; simply that if you want a high-quality service that goes beyond the regulatory minimum, and which is likely to deliver the results you want (value), you will have to pay for it. Think of the fees as part of your investment: a great adviser will make you far more money over the years than they will cost in fees.

When it comes to my long-term financial future, quality and value are way more important to me than price. How much is your financial future worth to you?

Wrapped in Red Tape

We must strike a balance, and to some extent that's what regulation is for. Look at the big banks for example. They were largely responsible for the 2008 financial crash, and we still bailed them out with public money. Those same institutions then resisted some of the changes introduced to ring-fence their retail banking operations and protect public money from their higher-risk investment and derivative operations.

Ultimately, there were two factors at play in 2008: corporate greed driven by a political system that courted and encouraged city excesses as it was driving economic growth—all in the name of re-election. There was also a failure of regulation.

We've gone a bit too far the other way now; in my specific niche, within financial services for individuals and business owners, the amount of regulation, administration, regulatory reporting, and red tape is stifling and expensive.

It's an area most clients don't understand—and why would they? Non-experts should be able to trust experts to keep you safe from those who would take advantage of you. The cost of that trust—extra regulation—is borne by my business—and ultimately factored into my pricing.

The cost of Professional Indemnity Insurance is rocketing. We have to pay annual levies to the FCA to fund the Financial Services Compensation Scheme. It might be a government scheme, but it's paid for by the industry—which means it's actually paid for by you through our prices. We have to provide complex reporting to the FCA about the products we sell, how many of them we shift, and the income we generate. It's expensive to produce those reports and ensure accuracy.

And yet there remain clients who think it's okay to pay less than everyone else, who want to pay the lowest price possible, regardless of the consequences. Leaving aside the consequences to advisers (not being able to afford to run their businesses) there's no way such clients will get top-class service.

The challenge for my industry (and it's the same for most industries, to be fair) is demonstrating value to potential clients. Showing value is remarkably hard to do when the law requires us to present information in a confusing way. The regulator and the industry do actually work hard to try to make it simple and easily understood, but I'm not convinced they've been entirely successful.

However, there's plenty of research to show that financial advice benefits those who listen and take action. The International Longevity Centre, supported by Royal London, found those who received financial advice in the period 2001-2007 accumulated significantly more liquid financial assets and pension wealth than their unadvised peers by 2012-2014. The "affluent but advised" group in their research accumulated on average 17% more in liquid financial assets than their non-advised peer group.[3]

A report by Unbiased[4] rounded up the research and also showed the benefits of ongoing financial advice. Retaining an advice relationship that consistently and regularly monitors and reviews your circumstances and objectives to ensure your money is always working as hard for you as possible.

Time In, Not Timing

Speaking of experts, it seems like they're everywhere. It's amazing how many people *just know* what's going to happen to house prices and the stock market. Most of them, however, are not experts and they're guessing. Like your mate Dodgy Dave down the pub.

Dave always has a share tip. You'd think he was a guru share trader by the amount of success he says he's had. He bought such-and-such and made £2,000 in a week. It's tempting to believe the egotistical bravado and dabble. Maybe you try to predict the best time to buy based on what Dave says and the *Mail on Sunday* stock tips column.

At first, you make a few quid, and it feels quite exciting. There's been a couple of investments that have done little, and some that went down. But the thrill of the ones that go up keeps you engaged. You're still only dabbling a few hundred quid; nothing you can't afford to lose.

Monday morning: oil crisis. The stock market falls 5%. It's had a big negative effect on your specific shares because of their link to oil. While the market may have fallen 5%, your shares have dropped 30%.

Ouch.

You dip your burnt fingers in some ice, sell the lot, and swear you'll never touch stocks and shares again.

Friday night. No sign of Dodgy Dave.

This is classic DIY investor behaviour. Buy when the market is rising and confidence is booming, then sell with fear as the market falls. Buy high, sell low. Short-term thinking. This is how it works. As the markets rise, consumer confidence grows and Dodgy Dave reports small wins. You feel optimistic and excited, but you're still uncertain.

The market continues rising and eventually you dabble, experiencing the thrill of gains followed by euphoria as you think you've beaten the markets. You're now at the point of maximum financial risk, when markets peak. As the market falls, anxiety and then denial set in; a temporary setback, you tell yourself, knowing full well you don't believe your own words. Then comes fear and desperation as you see your investment value disappearing before your eyes. Some people buy more at this point, in desperation. Others sell and make losses. With capitulation, comes panic and despondency as you accept that markets just aren't for you.

By this point, you're probably at the point of maximum financial opportunity with the markets at or near the bottom for that cycle. But you're still depressed because you've had a bumpy ride and had your fingers burnt. As the markets rise, feelings of hope and relief set in, before we're back to enough optimism that you buy in again.

In summary, you're trying to time the markets by buying in when you feel comfortable. The challenge is ignoring the crisis going on or just around the corner. It's easy to get caught up in the current crisis and allow it to affect your investment judgement. That's when people try to time the markets, thinking they can judge when the markets are at the bottom or top, and when to buy and sell.

You can't. Nobody can. If you get it right, it's pure luck.

When Things Get Volatile

It's important to understand a little about how the markets work. When markets fall, prices become unstable because there's uncertainty and fear. This is called volatility and we can measure it. It's the measure of the rate of fluctuation of prices. The VIX® index is a good example of this.

In early March 2020, as stock prices plummeted with an oil crisis and COVID-19, the VIX shot up. The market was twice as volatile as any time in the preceding nine years. When the volatility measures go up, automated selling algorithms kick in. So, what you see is an external event jitters market confidence and causes investors to sell. This increases volatility. This causes the automated selling algorithms to kick in—which further deflates prices. It's a perfect storm that drives the stock market down.

And guess what? The DIY investor wakes up to see their

shares plummeting and runs for the hills. They often sell immediately, crystallising their losses. When we ask these same people when they will buy again, they usually answer with, "When prices are going back up." By which time they've missed the boat by trying to time the market. They've waited until the market has already risen again before they buy back in. This is because they are making emotional decisions. They've actively decided to sell low and buy high.

Never in human history has this ever been a successful investment strategy. It is an extremely fast way to set fire to your money, though.

In late 2018 a couple who already had a financial adviser approached me. The market was falling, and they'd stopped making their pension and investment contributions as they "didn't want to lose any more" by seeing the new investment fall too. This is a classic investor emotional reaction. With a decade or more until retirement, time was on their side—yet they'd made an (unadvised) active choice to stop buying at cheaper prices and wait until it was more expensive again. All else being equal, the right long-term course of action was to continue investing.

There is also an argument to invest more, if you can afford it, when prices fall dramatically. I gave them the same advice they were already receiving: ignore the short-term noise and stay focused on the long-term objective. You can't time the markets.

Little and Often Wins the Race

The second aspect of the emotional investor story is frequency. It's better to make regular smaller contributions than infrequent lump sums. This is because we buy at multiple different prices, which smooths out natural volatility over the long-term. It smooths our return and feels less scary. So, when markets fall, you're still buying—and the savings you make will cover any expensive purchases made when the markets rise again.

Tied to the concept of little and often is compound interest. Albert Einstein wrote, "Compound interest is the eighth wonder of the world. He who understands it, earns it; he who doesn't, pays it."

So, how does it work?

In simple terms, you earn interest upon interest upon interest. Your interest snowballs. It compounds. The earlier you make your investment, the greater the benefit of compound interest.

Let's consider how this works. If you have £100 saved and you earn 5% interest every year, in one year's time you will have £105. At the start of year two, you now have £105 invested which grows at 5% so at the end of year two you will have £110.25 and so on. In 10 years' time, you will have £162.89. So, if you wait 10 years and then put £100 into savings, you have missed out on £62.89 of interest. That's 63% growth lost.

You can see the effect this has in the diagram below. Sarah and Larry are twins. Sarah is sensible, Larry is not. Sarah saves £200 per month for 10 years from age 35 to age 45 and then leaves it invested. Larry also saves £200 per month, but he starts at age 45 and saves for 20 years until age 65. Sarah has saved £24,000 whilst Larry has saved £48,000, twice as much as Sarah. Yet, by age 65, they both have virtually the same amount of money invested. Sarah has £85,000 because of the power of compound interest and Larry has £83,000.[5]

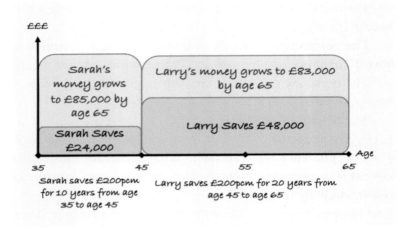

££€

Sarah's money grows to £85,000 by age 65

Larry's money grows to £83,000 by age 65

Sarah Saves £24,000

Larry Saves £48,000

Age

35   45   55   65

Sarah saves £200pcm for 10 years from age 35 to age 45

Larry saves £200pcm for 20 years from age 45 to age 65

The 8th Wonder of the World: Compound Interest

It costs Larry twice as much to retire with roughly the same as Sarah, just because he waited 10 years to invest. The earlier you start the better. Let's look at another example.

Let's say you want to have £1 million in your pension pot at age 65.[6] At birth, if you invest a lump sum of £42,000, you could have £1 million at age 65. Wait until you're 40, though, and you need to invest £295,000. Wait until you're 50, and your investment needs to be £481,000. Eye-watering sums.

Similarly, if you instead invested £175 per month from birth to age 65, you could have £1 million at age 65. It would have cost you just £136,500 to put £1 million away for your retirement. I'll take that any day.

If you start investing at age 18, you would need to invest £444 per month.

From age 30, you would need to invest £870 per month.

From age 40, you would need to invest £1,630 per month.

From age 50, you would need to invest £3,525 per month.

So, the person who saves from birth had to save just £136,500 over 65 years to have £1m at age 65.

The person who started at age 18 had to save £250,000 to have £1m at age 65.

The person who started at age 30 had to save £365,000 to have £1m at age 65.

The person who started at age 40 had to save £489,000 to have £1m at age 65.

The person who started at age 50 had to save £634,500 to have £1m at age 65.

The difference between saving from birth and saving from age 50 is a staggering £498,000. If you wait 50 years before you start saving for retirement, it'll cost you £500,000 more to save for your £1m retirement pot.

As a rule of thumb, £1 million at age 65-ish might generate a long-term retirement income of approximately £40,000 a year.[7]

Look at the difference. Absorb it. Then think about how much money you pissed up the wall in your twenties. I know I did. I learned a valuable lesson.

My kids already have pension accounts, and they're in primary school. They'll thank me when I'm long gone. The point I'm trying to make is: the small amounts you save in the first few years, they grow too. Interest, upon interest, upon interest. Growth, on growth, on growth. Compound.

I know £175 per month from birth might feel steep. So, start with £50. Or £10. Or even £5. *Anything*. Get started. Starting the savings habit is sometimes more important than the amount you save.

Your kids will thank you for it because the welfare state will not be there for them like it is for us and our parents. By the time our kids and grandkids get to retirement age, the state-funded retirement we know today will be very different. It's already barely enough to survive, and it's certainly not enough to live a fulfilling life. It is nothing more than a survival safety net.

In 50 years, will it exist at all?

Okay, so now we understand the power of saving early and how time is your friend, let's look at strategies you can employ to start the early savings habit.

Let's say you've committed to put £20 a month into a pension for your kids. That's £20 of your own money. Woo hoo, £20 for the kids. Actually, no. That's £25 for the kids.

Sorry, what? Where did the extra £5 come from?

Amazing, isn't it? You pay £20 into a pension for the kids and another £5 appears by magic—and it didn't cost you a penny. It's called tax relief. At the time of writing, the government adds a further 25% into the kids' pension for you. OMG. Seriously.

So that £175 a month from birth we talked about above, actually only costs you, the parent (or lovely grandparent), £140 a month. That's £35 a month for free. What's more, that £35 a month grows for free because there's no tax payable on the growth of money in a pension.[8] It's free money.

My youngest child, currently eight, sits down with me monthly to review his pension and Junior ISA investment performance. We talk about how much money he has in his money box, and how he'll be able to buy less stuff with it next year. We talk about what he's saving up for, if anything, and we talk about what his pension is invested in and what that means for his future.

We take his historic investment performance number, a percentage annual growth rate we've achieved over the first eight years, and we model that forward to his earliest retirement age (55 currently, but due to rise) and to age 18 for his Junior ISA. I say *we*; I do it. I work out how much his existing pension will be worth at retirement age assuming the return he has made continues at the eight-year historic rate minus 2% for inflation.

It's a bit rough and ready, but it's big numbers and he likes it. He's always asking me to put a few pounds from his money box into his pension because he knows and understands that it "instantly" grows by 25%. He can see the potential future value when he retires. It's quite a few Bugattis.

My older child, who's currently eleven, just wants to spend his money now. I can explain this stuff until I'm blue in the face, but he still wants his cake today. It's amazing how different they are. I remain hopeful he will make some sensible investment decisions!

What's Next?

Unless you're confident you know what you're doing, get professional advice to invest your hard-earned money.

1. Write down your top 3-5 financial objectives from an investment point of view. For example, retire at 65 with a joint income of £50,000, or pay for school fees.
2. Next to each objective, list the financial resources you've already accumulated to meet that objective such as the value of existing pension funds, the value of your business, a second property or savings.
3. How big is the gap between existing resources and your objective and how long do you have to close the gaps?
4. Formulate a plan to close the investment gaps and monitor progress every year to make sure you stay on track.

15

THE FINANCIAL NAVIGATOR

"THE BEST TIME TO PLANT A TREE WAS 20 YEARS AGO. THE SECOND-BEST TIME IS NOW."

Your financial prosperity is like a tree. The longer you leave it, the faster it needs to grow to provide the shade you're looking for, and the more it'll cost you (remember those calculations we did in the previous chapter?) As Warren Buffett said, "Someone's sitting in the shade today because someone planted a tree a long time ago." If you want to sit in the shade and enjoy the fruits of your labour, then you need to plant the tree right now. If you don't, you'll have no shade to protect you from the scorching sun.

That's as long as you don't live in the UK. If you live in the UK, you'll be looking for the tree to provide shelter from the howling wind and rain.

I get it though. It feels scary to plant the tree, to commit to action. At first, you can still move the tree when it's a young sapling, as long as you take care and seek expert advice. But as it gets bigger, it gets harder to move until eventually all you can really do is keep it neatly trimmed.

It's not much different in my world, but at some point you need to commit to the long-term provision of shade (shelter).

When it comes to commitment, my wife holds the world record for procrastination and indecision. She has made it into an art form, of which I am proud, because it tempers my natural exuberance. This means we have a sort of plan for things, which evolves as we go. Kind of like having a financial strategy and adjusting things as you go along. Sound familiar?!

But at some point you have to commit. Now, you can commit wholeheartedly with no going back, or you can do enough to get going and let the decisions flow naturally. The second method is what we do at home.

Beverley isn't so good at visualising how things might look, so plans for major works at home or in the garden are fluid. It took me some time to get used to this way of working as it's not my natural state. When we decided to build a new driveway and carport, rather than draw up fully detailed plans and have someone execute them for us, we chose to do it ourselves so we could design as we went. We had an overarching plan and the key elements set, but the finesse and detail of the curves and placement were fluid and we made decisions as we went along.

So, I bought a used JCB and had it shipped from Germany. As you do. I don't think we're normal. Who else buys a JCB to make their own driveway?

Sometimes you just need to take the plunge and do it. Commit to action and make it happen.

The 18-Minute ISA

I live a very privileged life. I don't mean that in the sense of being born with a silver spoon in my mouth; I mean I get to live inside my clients' lives as their trusted adviser, confidant, and mentor. It is a genuine privilege to know and understand my clients' dreams, goals, and aspirations. It's a genuine privilege to help, to give them peace of mind, and a plan for their affluent prosperity. It comes with sadness too, at times, because things happen in my clients' lives which are sad for them: divorce, death, and illness, for example. Yet I remain by their side to help.

It's so much more than a job. It's my very existence. It's my why.

What does my help look like? What can you expect? How will it feel for you?

I can't answer that last question, but I can certainly answer the first two which is what this chapter is all about. What can you expect from The Financial Navigator and how is that different to everyone else?

I used to run my business under the umbrella of one of the UK's largest wealth management organisations until I felt disenchanted. I spent several months researching alternative options, during which I spoke to many organisations and other advisers about what they offer and their experiences. The thing that stood out most was the transactional nature of most of the advisers I spoke to. One of them was proud to tell me how he could bring a new client on with an ISA investment in 18 minutes. I was appalled. How can you possibly know and understand your client in 18 minutes? That is not what I do.

Discovery

Discovery is a big part of my why (and my life). I like to discover new things. I like to experience new things. I like to try new things and have fun with life. I don't hire someone with a JCB to dig out my new driveway—I buy a used JCB and have fun doing it myself.

You'll see what I mean by discovery when you book an initial Discovery Call with me. We'll start by discovering the problems you're experiencing, focus on your biggest financial challenge, and understand why you're taking this step now, and why with me. The purpose is to see if I can help you, whether we're a good fit for each other, how committed you are to the process, and to explain how we work.

You might not like what you hear and decide working with me isn't for you, and that's okay. Equally, I may decide that I can't or don't want to help you. If that's the case, I'll point you toward someone who can help you, or some resources that will help. This isn't because I dislike people; it's because I can't help everyone.

And it's because the success of the advice I give depends on the amount of effort you put in. You can't outsource figuring out what you want to do and when; you can't outsource your goals and objectives. This means there is work for you to do. You need to be as committed to providing information and making decisions in a timely manner as I am committed to creating, executing, and monitoring a financial strategy for you. Maybe I can help you, but not yet. There may be things you need to do before I can really make a difference in your life. I'll tell you if that's the case.

Working with me is a partnership. We have to work together and trust we'll both do what we say we're going to do. That's a really important value for me: integrity. If I say I'll do something by Thursday, you'll have it by Thursday. If something comes along to derail that, I'll reset the expectation; you'll certainly not be chasing me on Friday.

It applies the other way around too. I'm not interested in constantly chasing clients for information or signatures. It's a waste of my time and it impacts other clients because I have less time for those clients who do prioritise their affluent prosperity.

If you're not a doer, it'll not work out for us to work together. I design my processes to identify people who don't do as they say, so that neither of us wastes our time. I'm like Ronseal: I say what I mean, and I mean what I say, and then I do it.

Some people find me direct—and it's certainly the case that whilst I enjoy a good chat, I also like to get on with the purpose of the meeting. It means I'll tell you what you *need* to hear and not necessarily what you want to hear. If you've been a wally, I'll tell you. So, if you're looking for empathetic sympathy every time you fail to do what you said you were going to do, you probably won't like me. And I'm perfectly okay with that because I'm not looking for anyone's approval. I'm interested in making sure you take the right actions to create the affluent prosperity you deserve.

If you're serious about your financial prosperity, though, if you're prepared to roll your sleeves up and work hard for the future of your family and business, then we'll make things happen.

I remember having a reputation in flying training for being "curt" in the cockpit. Nobody took umbrage to it because I was really (really) good at my job. Most people enjoyed knowing exactly where they stood and what was going on. If I was busy working out missile trajectories and positioning, and someone asked a question, I'd just say "Wait." Others might interrupt their flow or respond with something gentler like, "Would you mind holding on a minute please." Stuff that. There ain't no time for pleasantries when you're fighting a war!

As a crew, we work hard to understand each other, to maximise the efficiency of the machine. In the cockpit, it means knowing when to ask a question and when to shut up. It means knowing with absolute confidence and clarity that when something goes wrong, the only person you want sitting next to you *is* the person sitting next to you. Serving in the Arabian Gulf, Sam and I had that complete and utter trust. When we were flying that machine, it wasn't two individuals doing their individual roles, it was two people acting in unison to keep us safe, to keep the ship safe, and to carry out our mission.

If that sounds melodramatic or trite, it's not meant to; but the same principle applies to my client relationships. The trust goes both ways. I need to know my clients will do what they say they're going to do, particularly if there's a time limit or a deadline we have to hit. My clients need to know their affluent prosperity is in safe hands.

That is the purpose of Discovery. Knowing me; knowing you. (A-ha.)

Strategy Creation, Research, and Adoption

So, we've discovered synergy between what I offer and what you're looking for, and we've decided we're going to crew up to deliver your affluent prosperity. That's brilliant. It gets me really excited.

I love strategy creation. I love the mystery that comes with understanding your circumstances, helping you figure out what's important to you, and why. I love distilling the messy into the clean, because most client's financial lives are messy when we first meet. Most people don't know what they want, they don't know where they're going, and they don't know when. And it's okay not to know, because figuring that out is what I do.

I'll get inside your hopes and dreams to understand your why. You might not always know that yet, but that's okay. The very process of discussing it is strangely revealing. I've never worked with a client who hasn't enjoyed the experience of actually writing down and drawing out where they are today, where they want to be, and any specific goals they might have. This process forms the basis of your plan for financial prosperity.

After all, the definition of affluent prosperity and personal sovereignty is having the time and money to choose what you want to do and how you'll achieve your life goals.

It takes a joint effort to get your financial arse moving. A joint effort up-front to kick-start financial momentum for your affluent prosperity. As Abraham Lincoln said, "Give me six hours to chop down a tree and I will spend the first four sharpening the axe." You need to prepare for your action. You don't rush headlong into it.

Putting the financial plan together can feel like herding cats sometimes, particularly for me as I co-ordinate all the various elements into a financial strategy that delivers your affluent prosperity.

You're not the cat, by the way, it's the various financial product providers I have to deal with, all of whom have different requirements, different systems, and different processes.

But there is work for you to do, too. The quality of my advice is based wholly on the quality of the information you provide. I don't know what you have today. I don't know what you earn and spend. I don't know how many pensions you have. I don't know what's in your head. I don't know how much risk you're prepared to take. All these things need your input, which is why I look for commitment at the Discovery stage. I can't do this alone, and nor can you. We've chosen to work as a crew which means we both have to take part and pull our weight.

We'll also be reliant on others outside our control, to provide their services efficiently and effectively. With the best will in the world, that doesn't always happen. This means it can take time to get the information we need to give you expert advice. I can't just pick up the telephone to your existing pension provider and ask them some technical details I need to know. I don't have the authority to do that, and they have a duty to protect your information. We'll need letters signing and we'll be beholden to the timescales of others sometimes. Some providers still insist on your signature on an actual piece of paper, too. How quaint!

The outcome of our work together will be your tailor-made financial strategy for your affluent prosperity. It'll set out your hopes and dreams, your goals and expectations, what's important to you and why. We'll both commit to making it happen. We'll adopt it as your plan for affluent prosperity.

Time spent now will pay dividends later, giving you sustainable wealth, a richer lifestyle, and an enduring legacy with less hassle, and less work.

Implementation

 "You can't plough a field simply by turning it over in your mind." Gordon B. Hinckley

Now we've created your financial strategy, we'll put it into action. We'll start ploughing the field, chopping the tree. I like this part, too, because we're putting the building blocks in place to implement your financial strategy and deliver your affluent prosperity.

We might not do everything at once.

We might ease into your plan because it may be completely new to you, and scary. That's okay. That's part of the strategy, because your plan will say when we're going to do particular things, and why.

We might implement some aspects before we fully adopt the strategy. It's not a completely linear process; there will be some overlap because there may be some quick wins we can do straight away.

This is the exciting part. We get to *do* something rather than just talk about what we're going to do. You commit to your plan and you commit to be held accountable for it. I'll hold you accountable. If your plan calls for you to increase profits by 20%, I'll be checking (and helping) you do exactly that. If your plan calls for you to make a particular decision in six months, I'll be checking (and helping) you do that. If the plan calls for me to review your position on a six-monthly basis, I'll do that too.

There's a lot of work for me to do behind the scenes, mostly of a regulatory and administrative nature, to make sure we take the right actions at the right time. It will require some input from you, mostly to sign and agree to terms and conditions and, of course, to make your investment contributions. That's the important bit—the real commitment from you—getting your money working for your affluent prosperity.

I'll maintain a full record of exactly what money you have and with whom. You'll be able to see this through our client portal, providing you with access to daily valuations and information about your investments. However, I don't encourage my clients to spend much time there because it leads to short-term thinking. The daily fluctuations in price hide the long-term trend, and it is the long-term outlook we're interested in.

Be patient and you will be rewarded.

Financial Navigation

When you have a child, it doesn't end there. They grow up. They turn into grumpy teenagers (I have that to come) and they need different things at different times. We have to think about the best course of action. Sometimes the best course of action is inaction (you have to pick your battles with teenagers) and sometimes it's action (you're grounded for a month).

Being a parent is all about the changes, the journey. It's about how we navigate the challenge of parenting because it doesn't come with an instruction manual. So, what do we do? We seek advice. It's the same with your financial strategy. It needs to be nurtured and cared for. It needs to be reviewed and monitored. It needs to be tweaked and adjusted, fine-tuned like a piano or guitar. Get it right, and it's music to your ears; leave it too long and you'll know about it when you tinkle the ivories.

Leave it long enough and your Chopin will sound like nails down a blackboard.

Nobody wants to get to retirement, or whatever goal you set, to find the carefully crafted strategy has gone off track. The ship needs to be steered constantly. When the sea is calm, it needs less attention than during a storm, but it still needs attention.

Things will change in your life, too, and they will have a material effect on your strategy. If you want to stay the course, you need to keep steering the ship. It's really important that you don't just start the engine and forget it.

For example, let's say you have some of your money in a medium-risk ISA for long-term savings to support retirement. It might be invested in cash and nine different funds ranging from low-risk, low-interest Government bonds right through to funds investing in high-risk Far East emerging markets. Overall, your portfolio will be medium-risk. For argument's sake, let's say you have 10% in each fund and 10% in cash. Call it £10,000 in each.

Your funds grow at different rates. The effect of your low-risk funds growing by less than your high-risk funds is that the overall risk can naturally increase. Without being aware of it, you can approach your goal when your risk appetite for the money you have saved for that goal is lower—but the total investment is running at a much higher risk than you think. Just because you invested at medium risk doesn't mean it stays that way. Your portfolio might now be upper-medium or higher risk depending on how each fund has performed and how long you've left the ship unattended.

Which is why it's important to review your investments.

Your natural risk appetite changes, too. When you're 35 with 30-plus years to go until retirement, you're young and carefree and you have plenty of time on your hands, so you can afford to take more risks with your investments. As you approach retirement, though, and you've built a substantial nest egg, you'll naturally want to take less risk because the impact of a large drop in value just before retirement is significant.

This means we need to review your natural risk appetite for your particular goal—and potentially change the investment mix to match your changing risk appetite.

And what about what you've invested in? Has the fund manager changed? Has something happened in that industry or geography that doesn't fit with your attitudes and beliefs? Has something changed in that fund which gives cause for concern about its future prospects? These are the questions we ask when we review investments to determine whether they remain the right investment for you.

There's also legislation and taxation to keep on top of. These change constantly. Thankfully, I really enjoy this part too. You probably think I'm weird: you're right. I am weird and I'm damn proud of it too! I love and embrace my quirky self with joy. The fact that I love it means I'm very thorough, which means you're in safe hands.

The point I'm making is that investment isn't a one-off activity that you do just once and leave it. The true value of the work we do is in making sure your strategy stays right for you, in making sure you continue to make headway towards your goals, in steering the ship. Because life changes.

Make a Commitment

Commitment. It's a scary word for some people, others take a gung-ho attitude. Whichever way you look at it, we have to start somewhere. You can choose to bury your head in the sand and hope for the best. You can choose to plant the tree next year. You can choose sun over shade, rain over shelter. That's up to you.

But I do know this: the longer you leave planning for your financial future, the harder it gets.

194 FIND IT. GROW IT. KEEP IT.

It all starts with a conversation. That's not too hard, right? There's no commitment, no sales pitch, no pushy language, no confusing lingo—just a conversation about you, me, and what to expect.

And then you decide what to do next. It's up to you. All I ask is you don't leave it too late and end up with regrets, whether you work with me or someone else.

Remember: the best time to plant a tree is 20 years ago; the second best time is now. Let's get started.

16

CONCLUSION: A GROWTH MINDSET

MINDSET WILL LARGELY DETERMINE YOUR LEVEL OF SUCCESS OR FAILURE—WHAT'S YOURS?

Mindset has been a major theme in my book, for good reason. A strong and positive mindset is essential for developing and maintaining healthy self-esteem. By which I mean enough, but not too much. Too much self-esteem leads to misplaced arrogance. Healthy self-esteem means our internal stories, the words we say to ourselves, our mindset, is positive and encourages us to excel by reinforcing positive attitudes, beliefs, and feelings about ourselves.

Carol Dweck, a Stanford psychologist, talks about fixed and growth mindsets. Someone with a fixed mindset believes they were born with a certain amount of intelligence and talent which is unchangeable. Those with a growth mindset, however, believe intelligence and talent can be developed and strengthened through commitment and hard work.

I definitely have a growth mindset.

When it comes to your business and your life choices, your mindset will largely determine your level of success or failure, no matter where you come from. It will determine your resilience and how much you persevere in the face of setbacks.

Dweck writes that those with a fixed mindset tend to seek approval. She says, "I've seen so many people with this one consuming goal of proving themselves in the classroom, in their careers, and in their relationships. Every situation calls for a confirmation of their intelligence, personality, or character. Every situation is evaluated: Will I succeed or fail? Will I look smart or dumb? Will I be accepted or rejected? Will I feel like a winner or a loser?"

Reflecting on the stories in this book, you can see how a fixed mindset is often aligned with ego and approval-seeking, whereas a growth mindset is grounded in hunger for learning, for growth. Those with a growth mindset don't view failure as a disappointment. They see it as a learning experience, as an experiment that leads to personal growth and development.

Find It

A growth mindset focuses on learning, growing, and developing, rather than the result. It's about the experience, not the outcome. This ties back to measuring the success of your thoughts, beliefs, and actions with results. The focus is not on the result because that is out of your control.

You can use this idea with your kids to help them develop a growth mindset. Instead of telling children how clever they are, instead we can positively comment on their effort, their determination, and the process they used to get the result. It's not about the mark they get, but how they do the work.

You will need resilience in your business if you're to achieve personal sovereignty and affluent prosperity, if you are to find sustainable wealth, a richer lifestyle, and an enduring legacy. It will not happen by accident!

You will face setbacks. You will lose clients when you instigate your rules, because some of them will not like it. And that's okay. It's your business and you need to take charge of it.

Remember, most people are wandering around with an umbilical cord in their hands looking for somewhere to plug it in. It's your job to offer your plug socket to their umbilical cord and see if it fits.

Whatever you do, don't offer a travel adaptor to fit every need. You have one plug that describes you and your business. It either fits or it doesn't. Trying to fit a square plug in a round hole will not work, so don't do it.

Throughout this book, I've introduced some core financial ideas which you'll need to develop your business into the rip-roaring profit-making machine it can be. This starts with knowing your numbers. I know that feels scary. I know that may not be something you want to do. But that's why good accountants exist, to distil complex data into simple and useful information you can use to understand your business performance and measure the success of your processes. If your accountant isn't up to the job, please find a new one.

Evolution, Not Revolution

Your personal and business processes are the key to your growth success. With the ability to measure the success of your process, grounded in knowing your numbers, you have the means to continuously improve by driving process efficiency and profitability. But you do need a plan.

You can't do everything at once and even if you could, it wouldn't be helpful to you, anyway. Imagine making 16 different changes to your process and seeing a 6% improvement in efficiency. But which change made the positive difference? If you'd only done 12 of them, would that 6% be 8% instead? And which 12 changes would have done it?

It's important to consider and plan process improvements, prioritising those changes that'll bring you the biggest bang for your buck, and making sure you design the measures you need to prove, or disprove success. I know this can feel overwhelming. I've been there with my own business transformation.

Where do you start? Like any journey, it starts with a step. One small step. Go back to Chapter 10 and start documenting your business processes using post-it notes and brown paper. Get organised by writing down all the ideas you have for process improvements, for working on the business, rather than in it. Get off the tools by delegating what you can to free up your time.

If you have staff, ask for their ideas. Put a process in place for them to write their ideas down to make things more efficient: you can discuss it together, then accept or reject it. Reward the best ideas that bring about the most improvement.

Develop a routine. Start today by setting aside one hour and writing down all the improvement ideas, or pitches, you can think of.

On Friday, spend an hour deciding which ones you're going to implement first. It might be one big idea; it might be several smaller ones. Then make it happen. Do the work to implement the change and measure any success. Remember, we're looking for evolution, not revolution.

Frequent small changes are far easier to measure and manage than large complex changes. In software development, they call this Agile. The principle is you spend week one understanding the business needs, week two designing the solution, weeks three and four coding the software, week five testing, and week six to implement the code change. You can apply this principle anywhere in business. One small change at a time. There are other benefits to making small changes, too: it's less scary and feels easier to undo if something goes wrong, and you get incremental and faster benefits in your business.

Build the Wall

That infamous Trump chant from the 2016 US Presidential election campaign is apt for your business, too. You're now taking charge of your business; business is improving, and the efficiencies are making a difference.

You're starting to see benefits. If you haven't already, it's time to build the wall. The emergency fund that keeps your business going when the inevitable shit happens. Because you now know your numbers (don't you), you know how much money you need in your emergency fund, so you've been working on it already. You've opened a bank account at a different bank, thrown away the cheque book and bank card, and you're building the funds you need to protect your business from stormy weather. You're doing the same with your personal finances too.

Remember, it's okay to keep your personal emergency fund as cash in the business as long as you account for the personal tax implications if you need it in a hurry. You can bet your bottom dollar you'll need it in the year when you've already drawn extra cash for the extension or the new car, so your personal tax rate will be higher.

Be careful here, because there can be unintended tax consequences when you take out large amounts of wonga in a tax year, typically more than £100,000. Seek professional advice to avoid making expensive mistakes. I've seen so many clients have to take out personal loans to pay the unexpected tax bill. It's not unexpected; it was unmanaged, and that's on you (and your accountant).

With the walls built, you need to keep out the rain. Both personally and in your business. If you have a business partner that isn't your spouse, ask yourself the hard questions. What happens to the business partner's shares in the business if they get seriously ill or die? Do you really want their spouse, child, parent, sibling, grandparent, aunt, uncle, or cousin in possession of their shares? That's what could happen without the right planning in place, according to the rules of intestacy (when you die without making a Will).

At home, is your family protected against the rain? Will you look down from your cloud knowing you've left them safe and financially secure? Or are you a tomorrow person? Nobody wants to see their spouse and children turfed out of their home at a time of immense grief, but that's what may happen if you don't put plans in place.

Make sure you have a rainy-day plan because it sure as hell rains a lot in England. As unpalatable as it sounds, the worst could happen to you.

Grow It

Woo hoo, you're making more money and you've created more time! Now for more choices.

More choices comes from securing your affluent prosperity, giving you the choice to work, to not work, to say no to less-than-perfect clients. To say yes to the things you want to do. To fulfil that bucket list. Go for more walks. Take more holidays. Travel. Excitement. To spend time with people you love doing things you enjoy. What better way to live your life?

It's time to grow your wealth. It's time to invest in your future prosperity. That might mean investing in your business to grow it, or it might mean investing profit in the markets. It might mean both, to spread the risk.

Just don't gamble it away.

When I ran my technology and business change consultancy before getting involved in financial services, I remember bumping into a former colleague who I thought had retired. In fact, he had retired in early 2008—but he had to come back to work. He was a DIY investor, and he hadn't understood investment risk and diversification. He'd happily been making high-risk investments and reaping the rewards, but he had no downside protection. He paid the ultimate price and lost most of it. He lost his money, and he lost his freedom because he thought he could do it himself.

He was your mate Dave down the pub.

Remember your three-legged stool? All three legs need to be firm. You need to build your emergency fund, mitigate the financial consequences of risk, and grow your wealth. You also need to keep it.

Keep It

Taxation takes money away from us. But managing taxation helps us keep as much of it as possible. This is one of the most complex areas to get right and you cannot possibly do it on your own. Your accountant should help with some of it, but in my experience, most accountants are not proactive at this. Giving you an avoidable tax bill isn't helpful. That's why you need to be on the front foot, to manage your income and profit, to look to the future to help you decide what to do now.

I think it was Nelson Mandela who said, "The shadow of the future is long." He meant that what you think the future is going to be, it's shadow, influences the decisions you make today. If you haven't a clue what the future might look like because you don't know your numbers, because you're not forecasting cash flow and profitability, then how can you make good decisions? Deciding to draw a large amount of profit from the business without considering your overall tax position and the timing of your income in the tax year, is a recipe for an unexpected and unpleasant bill. I've seen it, regularly.

I've also seen tax evasion. It's not big, and it's not clever. It's a crime. It's theft. I'm sure you wouldn't go into the bank and steal from the cashier, yet some people think it's okay to steal from you and me, via HMRC, by evading taxes that are legally due. The silly thing is, if they regularised their affairs and did things properly, with careful planning and efficient financial management they can often find themselves no worse off in terms of their overall wealth position. It's greed; a case of wanting their cake now. I understand why, but I will never condone or support such action.

I don't make the rules. I just operate within them. That means recommending the most tax efficient way to manage your finances to make the most of the rules. That's called tax efficiency, and it is perfectly legal. Tax evasion is not.

Let's Do It

I've done my bit. I've given you enough to take the steps you need to profit from your rip-roaringly successful business. I've given you tips and ideas to transform your business from a cash-eating monster to a profit machine.

If you can do it all on your own, I admire you, because most of us need support and accountability. I have accountability. I'm not on my own. I employ the services of a mentor and coach to make sure I do the right things at the right time in my business. To help me decide what my idea pitches need to be. To talk through a sticky problem. To tell me to stop being an idiot and just get on with it.

If you want to discover the secret wealth inside your business and navigate your way to affluent prosperity, find it, grow it and keep it, then visit my website at www.somersetwm. co.uk/contact and book a free Discovery Call to find out how I can help you do the things you need to do.

I've shown you the way. The rest is up to you.

AFTERWORD

Thank you. I just wanted to say thank you.

Thank you for taking the time to read my book. Thank you for taking the time to read my story and to think about how it may help you. Thank you for being interested in the hard work, tears, and tantrums that came with writing it. It means a great deal to me.

I said in the preface I wanted affluent prosperity and personal sovereignty, and I believe that is what we all seek and desire. We want sustainable wealth, a richer lifestyle, and an enduring legacy with less financial hassle. Less work. The freedom to choose what we do and when we do it. This passion underpins everything I do, be that in my business or my personal life. It's central to what this book is all about and it's central to my philosophy.

Personal sovereignty and affluent prosperity isn't all down to money, but getting your finances in order so your money works hard for you is a good first step.

I hope you derived value from reading it and I hope the information, stories, and tips help you get where you want to be.

I'd love to hear about your experience. I'd genuinely love

to hear from you, to understand what's changed for you since you read the book and implemented some ideas. I'd like to hear about what you've done or are doing differently and what difference this book has made for you.

Has your story changed? Do you see your business in a new positive light?

Send me an email and let me know. I always reply because I love hearing people's stories.

And finally, if you liked my book and you bought it from Amazon, please leave a review so it can help other people change their thinking, change their beliefs, and act differently to achieve the affluent prosperity they deserve.

Change only comes from commitment, so please commit to help others change with your review.

If you'd like to know more about what I do and how I do it, you can follow me on LinkedIn or sign up to email tips on my website at www.somersetwm.co.uk.

In the meantime, stay positive, stay focused and commit to action.

Do or do not. There is no try.

My very best wishes,

Nick

Nick Smith
The Financial Navigator
Find it. Grow it. Keep it.
nick@thefinancialnavigator.co.uk

ACKNOWLEDGEMENTS

Writing a book is not easy and I could not have done it without the support, encouragement and feedback of my family, friends, coaches and mentors.

Top of the list is my wife Beverley, and my children Monty and Roo, without whom I could not do what I do. Your unconditional love and support keep me going every single day. I love you and thank you. x

Special thanks to Vicky Quinn Fraser at Moxie Books who coached, cajoled, and guided me through the adventure of writing a book. You are very patient! Thank you.

I'd also like to say thank you to Jon McCulloch and Connor Benham for holding me accountable, for challenging me when I needed it, and for telling me to stop being an idiot when I needed to hear it. I will always appreciate your honesty. Thank you.

To Jules White, dragon slayer. Thank you for helping me understand and clearly articulate my why.

To my beta readers: Terry, Sarah, Charlotte, Anna, Simon, Chris, Tony, Jeremy, John, and Kevin. Thank you for putting up with a very raw copy of this book, before the professional edit. A proper copy is on its way to you.

Finally, to my long-suffering parents, constantly wondering what on earth I'm going to do next... I hope my children are a little less adventurous! Love you both x

APPENDIX

In Chapter 7, I wrote about how I found it quite difficult to decide on my rules, so I thought it might be helpful to include them below. It may trigger some thoughts of your own and help you think about your own frustrations which a rule may stop or mitigate.

But remember, these are my rules for my business. Your business is different, you are different, and your rules will no doubt be different.

Rule 1: I don't always answer the telephone

I don't answer the telephone when I am doing client work because I'm sure you would want me fully focused on your work. I ask my clients to book time in my diary using a private link to my calendar so I can give them the full attention they deserve and so I can be fully prepared for our discussion.

Rule 2: No-one gets my mobile number

There's a practical reason for this one. I need to keep clear call records about who called me when and whom I called, in case of complaints or if something were to happen to me. If that's happening across multiple telephone lines, it just gets harder, and therefore more costly to manage.

Secondly, for the same reason as not answering the telephone, interruptions distract from focus on the task at hand. It's about taking control of my time to be as effective and efficient for my clients as possible.

Rule 3: I'll not support debt to pay my fees

It would be professionally repugnant of me to advocate more debt to solve a financial problem. It's rarely the right thing to do.

Rule 4: No fat heads

This is a simple one. I only work with people I like. Egotistical fat heads need not apply.

Rule 5: Be respectful of people's time

As I respect other people's time by being on time, I ask the same of my clients. Remember, we're working as a crew, in this together. It's not a one-way street, it's a partnership and we both have our part to play.

Rule 6: My price is my price

If I bend on my price, what does that say about my integrity? It's also about value, quality and fairness to my clients who know, understand and appreciate the work I do.

Is it fair to my other clients that you pay a different price?

Rule 7: Courage

I have the courage to say what I mean and mean what I say. I'd like my clients to have the same courage. That means having the courage to pipe up with the stupid questions (there are no stupid questions, only stupid answers). It means having the courage to admit you don't understand something, and I need to explain it differently. Please do not sit in blissful ignorance.

Rule 8: Integrity

Doing the right thing. 'Nuff said.

Imagine: Unveil Our Truth

Close your eyes, imagine a place
A timeless place, of beauty beyond.

A garden of Eden, of pleasure and freedom
As pure as the virgin snow
As round and whole as the sun (we know)
As fresh as the wind does blow.

As crystal as pearls upon us rain
Each falling drop dissolving pain
Magic pearls that will never cease
Imagine this rain is a reign of peace.

Disposed at nature's will
Quiet, calm and statue still
An extinction of want a necessity of need
A place where this is no place for greed.

Of synchronised harmony undisturbed
Where the poisoned apple
And branch covered tree
Still grow together in unity.

Imagine this place and make it be
Now open your eyes and see.

Julian Smith © 1974-2006
Rest in Peace, my Brother.

ABOUT THE AUTHOR

When Vicky said I needed to write an "About the Author" section, I cringed. Isn't there enough of me in this book already without a few self-indulgent paragraphs about how wonderful I am? Yuck. No, thank you.

Vicky persuaded me otherwise, pointing out that readers like to know more because they're curious. But does anyone really care where I was born, where I grew up, and my favourite childhood pet? Rather than compose several autobiographical paragraphs, I thought I'd write 11 ever-so-slightly interesting things, in no particular order.

1. My first job before joining the Royal Navy was cutting the mould off enormous blocks of cheddar cheese. Fortunately, I love cheddar cheese.

2. My second job before joining the Royal Navy was manually checking the safety pop-up lids on 250,000 baby food jars. Tedious.

3. I drove from Weymouth to Portsmouth to join my first front-line ship, only to find the ship was in Plymouth. Oops.

4. I bought a bright orange VW Beetle the same age as me. Youthful.

5. I own a beautiful classic car, that belonged to my late brother. Her name is Mollie, and she is a 1966 Ford Anglia in the Harry Potter flying car blue.

6. I've been ballroom and Latin dancing, on and off,

since I was 20, and I once danced a waltz with Flavia Cacace from *Strictly Come Dancing*. She's really tiny.

7. I've seen a whale shark and her calf basking in the Arabian Gulf.
8. I flew over a pod of whales with their young in the Indian Ocean. It was a truly majestic sight.
9. I've seen thousands of turtles swimming round a tiny island off Kuwait.
10. My dog is called Bertie, and he is an adorable clown.
11. I dropped a live depth charge (underwater bomb) into the South China Sea, deliberately. It was past its use-by date! It made a very big splash.

www.thefinancialnavigator.co.uk

linkedin.com/in/thefinancialnavigator

NOTES

Introduction: Mayday! Mayday! Mayday!

1. You're probably slightly curious about the marketing element, so I'll explain. Everything we do is marketing in one form or another. Marketing of yourself, your ideas, your thoughts, your feelings. Every time you speak or act, you are seeking to persuade, which is all marketing really is. For the military, it means marketing our country. So yes, the military is also a marketing machine promoting UK plc's interests around the world, whether we agree with those interests or not.
2. Amazingly, the first car to pass by, screech to a stop, and run up to us wasn't the police. It was a passing news reporter. On page three of the *Scottish Sun* in mid-June 1997, in true tabloid exaggeration style, is a three-column inch article entitled "Navy helicopter crash-lands yards from houses."

1. Know Your Enemy

1. In case you're not a *Star Trek* fan like me, the Borg is an alien race whose sole aim is to forcibly assimilate other species into a collective, removing all traces of individuality.
2. www.nature.com/articles/s41562-018-0520-3

5. Discomfort and Grit

1. STAS stands for Short-Term Air Supply and it gives you about three minutes of air if your aircraft ditches in the sea.
2. Not his real name.
3. Take a look at this video if you want to learn more: www.youtube.com/watch?v=xXC6U0NfJg8

6. Rugged Individuals

1. Another great movie line, this time from *Pump up the Volume*.

8. Value and Worth

1. In it, a line of sheep following each other in single file fall off the edge of the cliff by blindly following the sheep in front of them.

12. Let's Talk About Risk

1. Data obtained from LV's Risk Reality Calculator on 3 Jan 2021 based on non-smokers: https://riskreality.co.uk/gen. "Couple" here means a male and female. The percentages refer to the risk happening to one of them.
2. Speaking of which, if physical health improvement is something you need help with, look up Phil Agostino and join his programme; he gets amazing results for his clients.
3. We could use a different age which would change the risk numbers, but the principle is the same.
4. A Trust is a legal arrangement where you give cash, property, or investments to someone else so they can look after them for the benefit of a third person. They are often used to manage Inheritance Tax on life insurance payouts.

13. Taxation and Bitter Pills

1. This is a complex area of tax legislation so make sure you take professional advice.

14. Wealth Excitement

1. Past performance is not a reliable indicator of future results.
2. A stochastic model is a tool for estimating probability distributions of potential outcomes by allowing for random variation in one or more inputs over time.
3. Read more about this research here: https://ilcuk.org.uk/the-value-of-financial-advice/
4. You can read the report here: www.unbiased.co.uk/news/financial-adviser/financial-advice-value-over-10-years
5. Assumes net real-term growth of 5% per annum.
6. Assuming net long-term real growth after inflation of 5% per annum.
7. Clearly dependent on investment performance!
8. There are other tax considerations in respect of when and how you access a pension, and the maximum amount you can have saved in a pension, which is why you should always seek expert advice because the rules change constantly.

BV - #0082 - 310821 - C0 - 216/138/10 - PB - 9781838385309 - Gloss Lamination